Midweek Moments
2017

Jane Wheeler

Published By:
Ray of Sunshine Ministries

Table of Contents

What If

Not that people are claiming or even throwing out days or dates, but I have been increasingly hearing different preachers and Bible teachers saying that 2017 looks to be a year like no other. What really does that mean?

With Donald Trump about to take over the White House - it definitely will be an interesting year. Donald tends not to be dull and boring.

I suppose it will be a year like no other because of the fact that it has not happened before. But what if....

What if ... this is the year Jesus comes back? Will you be ready?

Allow yourself to go there, what if.... you look into the sky and see a figure riding the clouds, angels riding along side. Every eye is upward, beholding the sight, every ear is tuned in to the thunderous noise the figures are making. You have been waiting for it, you knew it would come, but at this second, you wonder if you are ready... What if...

In the twinkling of an eye the whole world as you know it could change.

In your "what if" thinking, who comes to mind? Who should you go talk to? Who should you spend more time with? What priorities might change in your world if you thought this was really the year that life will change?

Even if Jesus does not come back - so many things can happen in one year or how about in one minute or in a day...

- you could lose a job or gain a job or promotion

- your family could suffer with relationship crisis or reunite after years of estrangement

- you could get a new family member by marriage or child birth or adoption

- you could loose a family member through sickness, death or divorce

- you could gain money or loose money this year

- you can become healthier or slide into unhealthy habits

- you can reside in the same home all of 2017 or move into a new home

So many things could happen - the answers are not ours to know ... just yet.

We live in anticipation that some things will occur in our life circle that will not be ours to control. We have been around this block enough times to know that life happens. How do we start 2017 well?

As my lovely grandma used to do to bring in the New Year - she would wait up until 12:00am every New Years and then go out to the front porch and bang pots and pans together yelling "Happy New Year". We would be allowed to wait up with her and head outside in our jammies and bang those pots and pans right alongside of her. By 12:07am we were tucked into bed and off to dream about the New Year.

We could spend January 1st declaring which things we wish to claim as our New Year's Resolutions - hoping this year our resolve will be strong enough to achieve them.

Some folks will spend January 1st sleeping in and slowly getting up since they partied too hard at the end of 2016.

No matter how we celebrate or ignore 2017 - it will slide into our lives and calendars, the date will quietly pop up onto our cell phones and computers, proclaiming itself to be here.

What if... good words to think about because you do not know what will happen this year, the news could be a phone call away, a week or a month away but news of some kind will come - good and bad. Let us live in expectation of the "what if's..." so that no matter what comes our way we will know we lived it well.

 Because in the end **you** are the only thing you can control.

Tech Savvy – Please Protect Yourself

It is a different world out there! No matter what we do we leave a trail, just like little red riding hood, and the big bad wolf is lurking at the door, just waiting....

I have been gleaning little bits of techie news and was not sure what to do with this info and then the light bulb went off – why not share this info on my blog.

A few years ago I trained with Volunteer Services with the RCMP. One of the requirements that both RCMP Members and Volunteer Services are given is that they are not allowed to be on Facebook. They told us that the info we put onto Facebook is not private. The basic concept is that Facebook gives you a piece of "real estate" on their site for free, and as we all know "free" is not really real in most things. Facebook uses your info and hackers use Facebook to get personal information about you. Do not put your real birthday or personal info onto Facebook. I found a lot of people did not believe me when I tried to share this but if you keep reading this is way bigger than that!

I am sure some of you are more technical savvy then myself so the info I share might not be totally new but I am hoping some of it is certainly helpful.

Another tip I got was from the school board techie guy who came out to rescue me in the library with a computer issue. He informed me how to know if a website is "secure" especially if it is for banking or paying info or buying products online.

I had always wondered why some websites started with **http://** and some started with **https://**. Well he informed me that the "**s**" means "secure".

 The other thing he pointed out was to look for the **little green padlock** before the https://. I was not even aware there was a little green padlock.

Both of those things mean the site is "secure".

He said that a true professional hacker can get into most anything but that websites with the "s" and "padlock" makes your personal information so scrambled it is almost impossible to decipher it.

Brian and I like to watch tv shows that portray the authorities able to track people and hack into their personal lives with ease. You hear rumors that this is "real" or the other rumor that no one can "possibly do that - it is just for tv."

I never really knew the answer until I watched a twenty minute video on CBC Marketplace - "*are your apps spying on you?*" January 6, 2017 episode, and then that most of us have even given them permission to do it!

WOW – what an eye opener – please for your personal and financial self – take the time to watch this video. ***Can hackers know all about you? - You Bet!*** They can take your picture with your own phone, they can listen in at any time, they can empty your bank account, lock you out of your own phone, house, car – depending what apps you have on your phone.

They do just that on the CBC Marketplace video - they did an experiment to see what kind of info they could randomly get - the results are shocking!

One of the current "trends" I heard about from the police is a term called "jacking". It is the current thing, hackers can access your phone and while they might not be able to get into your bank account – they will lock you out of your phone. Since many of us now turn our furnaces off/on with the phone, start our car, buy tickets, for a small fee the hackers will unlock your phone so you can regain access to your items. They basically hold your phone hostage until you pay.

There is no such thing as "free" apps: ask yourself why is a company giving me a "free" app? It comes with strings, Facebook, Twitter, Snap Chat, all of these have the ability to give out your information. Each of these apps comes with a Disclaimer, Contract, Legal Notice explaining what the company, who is providing the app, will do with your information. Most of us do not read those terms – hence the problem.

After watching the Marketplace video we were going through our phones. Brian wanted to know why his Sky View, a star watcher app needed access to his photos. We had not noticed this before.

Read on to find out why..

The other thing you need to know is that there is _no government legislation_ controlling this stuff, not in Canada.

Must watch Marketplace video: (copy this link and put it into the bar at the top of your computer) or you can look at the CBC Marketplace Facebook Page.

https://youtu.be/xx1AUupLn2w

Follow it up with a 2nd CBC Marketplace video on protecting your phone:

https://www.youtube.com/watch?v=QgwSz6PUxKo&feature=youtu.be

My son told me about a Documentary on Netflix called Citizenfour that is blowing the whistle on this kind of domestic spying being done by the USA's National Security Agency. Edward Snowden the whistle blower now has to live in Russia in fear for his life and threats from the US government.

Be Safe Everyone and Protect Yourself!

Not My Finest Hour

Our family of five, mom and dad and three boys, well we love nature. We were often out walking around in the forest, fishing, hunting, we liked to have fires out in the bush and cook hot dogs.

On this particular fall Sunday afternoon we were out walking in the bush, the boys were still in elementary school, so a long time ago, all of the sudden my husband said, "Stop."

The boys and I stopped and looked around, we did not see or hear anything, but he looked over at me and said "Get the boys back to the truck. Back up slowly and when you get about twenty yards away, just start running for the truck. There is a bear, I think it has been stalking us along the bush line."

I turned around and gave the boys my mom's in panic mode look and said, "Obey your father, NOW" and we turned around, walked roughly twenty yards and then made a bee line dash for the truck.

I got to the truck first, opened the door and told the boys to get in. When my boys caught up to me, one of them said, *"Thanks for saving us mom! You passed us back there and left us to get eaten."*

Realizing at that moment that I had actually done that, I had actually left my children behind to get eaten by the bear, and just ran and saved myself. I was horrified and humbled, truly not one of my finest moments.

That was over twenty something years ago and my boys still remind me about it: "Oh ya moms going to save us... remember the bear?"

So what exactly happened that day? Well, I think instinct, human instinct and self-preservation took over and I just ran. Oblivious to what was around me, I ran to save myself.

I think that is why God tells us we have to be so grounded in Him. We may not feel like reading our Bible, we may not feel like praying, or forgiving or .... but we need to because when life happens, human preservation, human instincts, take over. We will either turn to God for direction because it has been our habit to do so or we will try to save ourselves.

I am praying that now, since I have been a Christian for 30+ years, these principles are solidly grounded into me, so that if anyone today said "Run!" I would take the time to look around and see who I need to bring with me, *but you know* – it is the chance you take if you are going to *"run with me"*...

It's Semester Change

I have gotten to love my job in the library, I look forward to seeing "my kids" every day and talking with them. Oh there are still challenges but most days are pretty great.

I have this group of 7-8 kids who come on their spare and have gelled together into a really fun group. I relish sitting there listening to them talk and laugh, sometimes they play a game and other times they study together.

My "what's your chew" fellows have not been so regular but they were there last week and true to form they entertained me with their stories. The one fellow was obviously on a role to creep the girls out as he, in true redneck fashion, was discussing what kinds of animals he has "eaten"; apparently everything from bears to possums, even snakes. Like when he was 4 he got lost in the forest for 3 days and had to eat snake meat, he roasted it over the fire. _(I did not say any of this was true!)_ He told the girls that pet stores are really just a butcher shop in disguise, which did bring the disgust that he was looking for. When questioned if he ever had a "pet" he told us about his pet toad, it got really big holding his hands about a foot apart. His name was of course "toad" and it died because he kept forgetting to feed and water it.

My inside voice was questioning how "toady" got so big if he was that fat – but then I realized there probably never really was a "toad" pet, after all this boy was on a role.

Oh my – the stories!

Then there are the true and heart breaking stories.

One gal asked me what you say to your friend when she loses a baby.

What do you say to the young fellow who confides that he has no friends even when he seems surrounded by others.

Or to the young girl who you have never have seen talking to anyone else. She seems to have not one friend in the school and she sits alone lunch hour after lunch hour with a book hoping no one sees her or else wishes someone does!

Then there is the girl who tells you she has to do all the cooking and cleaning and watch her brother because her mom is not well and if her dad does not like supper he yells and gets mad – really mad.

Even though I did not want go back to work at the beginning of the year, my husband now teases me that I will miss these kids terribly when my contract is over (I am only covering a mat leave position til June). I am beginning to think he is correct.

But right now, this past and for the next couple weeks it has all changed. We are at exam time and schedules are up in the air and the kids are all stressed with exams and finishing up classes. I watched one fellow who finally applied himself get his marks from a 42% to 84% in one week all because he decided to finish some assignments. He has been hanging around the library trying to get to know a certain young lady putting his attention onto other matters.

Semester 2 starts February 1st, the whole dynamics of the library will be changed again, my regulars will be in different classes, no more spares. But with it will bring a new "group" of kids to the library, a part of me is excited to see who and a part of me roles my eyes with *oh boy – here we go again!*

Amazing How God Works

I remember when I was a brand new mom. Glen was only a few months old and I had been out digging in my garden in one of those rare mommy breaks, while he was napping. I was totally engrossed in my work and I was talking to God about life and specifically about Ladies Time Out. I had been in a group before I had the baby, but we had moved away from the group and I was in another church and another part of town. I was wondering about where the nearest group was so I could now attend as a "new mom" participant.

I distinctly heard God fill my mind with these words, "You start a group."

It was so incredulous and totally bizarre; I knew in my heart that my new role as "mom" was more important than anything else in the world, surely that was to be my focus and my only focus. Those words could *NOT* be for me. I mean I had put in my time, I had participated as a team leader at the other Time Out, it was my turn to go as a participant after all I had a new baby to take care of!

I actually looked over the fence I was working beside to see if God had missed His target and He was talking to someone on the other side. Low and behold, there was not a soul on the other side of the fence. Well He certainly could not have been talking to me.

Long story short – He was.

Even as I kicked and screamed and told Him it was not a very good idea, it was not fair, I had put in my time, it started my ten years as Ladies Time Out leader.

I find it amazing how God works, I think I have it all figured out and He shows up *never* according to my plans, or timing and He *never* seems to look at my organizational bullet points of how it should go! He floors me every time, and I *never* see it coming!

But this year, He gave me a hint. He has been pressing me that 2017 will be different, something is coming. He has confirmed it in several ways, through various people and to me personally. I do not know just what that means but I have a sense that it is going to be awesome.

Two weeks ago we had a phone conference with the Aglow Leadership, located all over Canada, these ladies heard from God that they were to come to Grande Prairie. Each one heard in a different way at a different time, but God told each one of them separately. Grande Prairie was the destination and from here they have been directed to go North to the NWT.

They are being obedient and coming: they have been given visions, prophetic words and messages that God is about to stir up the Peace Country. Can we call it a Revival? I do not know but what I do know is that God is confirming locally through other people and in other churches that He is up to something.

We are hosting an event in February, the 16, 17 called the "Northern Awakening Tour" with the Leadership of Aglow. We are going to be prepared to see what God does and how He shows up.

I know many churches have been praying for a Revival for years. I had not sensed anything about a Revival I was sensing more that 2017 will be a year unlike any other we have had.

I have heard about a few other churches and Christians who have the same sense that God is about to do something big in Grande Prairie. He is calling believers to get ready to be prepared to see Him do a mighty movement of some kind.

As I was driving home this evening the Northern Lights came alive before me in the sky, dancing and shimmering above the horizon. It was breathtaking. I watched as the lights moved back and forth, sparking high into the sky and then back down again.

I told God that He did good work! As I got nearer to the city, the lights began to fade, the more buildings the more lights, the dimmer the Northern Lights got. It was not that they were not out just that the other lights drowned out their brilliance.

A lot like our relationship with God, a lot of other things distract us from seeing the true Light. The more artificial light we have on, the less we see the true Light.

Will we be ready to see God move around the Peace Country? Not unless we turn off some of the lights. Not unless the distractions around us fade. Think about it, tv is a form of light, our phones are a source of light, computers shine their own light...what other lights might be distracting us?

God is calling, stirring and shaking the hearts of His people to get ready, will it be just for this one event? I doubt it- when God starts working it is usually not isolated, He has a much bigger picture in mind. But I for one do not want to miss it.

Why Grande Prairie? In a blog last year (True North Strong and Free) I gave the disturbing statistic that

Grande Prairie had been named the Crime Capitol of Canada. Where else would you bring the light – except to the darkest place? The light shines the brightest in the dark.

Are you ready for Him to light us up?

What if we today after reading this blog, we go back to our very roots – to our childhood and start singing and humming a song – *This Little Light of Mine* for the rest of today and the rest of this week maybe even for the rest of the month.

You see wherever you are, in the Peace Country, east coast, USA – God is wanting to use you. When you purposely decide to let your light shine for Him, His light has already begun to glow. The darkness is receding, just like the Northern Lights dancing on the horizon, we all will be streams of light being sent into remote and dark places that God has designed just for you to enter into and shine on people whose lives you are touch.

Will you join Him?

Life's Eruptions

Eruption: Definition mine: Blow the top off and/or release a flow of lava = life disruption to the world around it.

I am wondering how your section of the world has been this week, mine has been intense.

I do not mean just for me personally, it definitely has been, but for others around me too and I knew that something in the spiritual realm was moving.

Let me give you a brief recap of the week as I encountered it:

Me: bronchitis, pneumonia, I reacted to 2 types of medications badly, sleepless nights, violent barfing, one night I seriously questioned God if He was going to take me as I woke up with a heart rate that I think was off the charts. I have slept, drank more liquid than probably most fish ever do in their lifetime. I have this week felt the "eruption" of sickness.

Other people very close to me, that my heart aches for, had their own storms:
- Surgeries, blackouts and seizures, life and death incidents, sickness, heart and kidney issues, babies possibly 10 weeks early.

How was your week?

I asked God about all the above incidents and what they were about. I got a visual and it might take a bit of explaining...........

Picture: *hash browns in frying pan*
Okay, we are truly not "hash browns" to God but this is the visual He gave me and then He told me that He started to "shake" the pan.

You know what happens when the pan shakes? Our world as we know it starts shaking, moving and often turning upside down; the mountains seem way taller than we can climb. The pan itself stays firm but the insides rock and roll.

Yesterday, physically, I did not know what to do. The medication was not working, again, I had been violently sick (vomiting) all morning, I could not breathe, my head was so plugged I thought it might explode and I was physically spent. Nothing seemed to be working, I had a Dr. appointment at 1:30.

At 1:00, I was presented with a song by Sheri Easter, *Praise His Name.*

I sat on my bed and sobbed and snotted through the song and raised my hands in Praise and tried to cough and sing my way through. It was in those moments I realized God was very smart, crying was beginning to release a lot of pressure in my head and I knew somewhere through the 3 times I played the song. God and God only started to heal me.

It was not the crying – it was the Praise.

When I got to the Dr. he said my lungs were sounding better – A God Miracle cause I was wheezing in the morning.

Praise is one of the Keys to Gods Kingdom.

Other countries get this way better than we do in North America. In countries so poor that we seem like millionaires they 'out praise' us a hundred fold. I remember listening to the *Keepers of the Faith*, a Samoan singing group who actually told the audience that he hates singing in North America because we do not get it. They had performed the week before in a country just ravished by a hurricane but the people *PRAISED GOD* for His faithfulness! They had nothing and they Praised, we have so much and have a hard time doing it.

I read a quote in a novel that sealed what I was thinking: *"You know, my people were praising in the slave cabins long before their circumstances changed. They praised by faith and so must you...."* The List, Robert Whitlow

Slaves Praising God and we all know Black folks *KNOW* how to Praise! But they learned to Praise *Before* They Saw the Results.

In the Bible, Paul and Silas in prison Praising God. "About midnight Paul and Silas were praying and singing hymns to God, and the other prisoners were listening to them. Suddenly there was such a violent earthquake that the foundations of the prison were shaken. At once all the prison doors flew open, and everyone's chains came loose" Acts 16:25,26

Our circumstances in life can be so huge and overwhelming and not in the least trivial. They chain and hold us down under their weight and they threaten to overtake us, and yet God says to Praise Him.

I mean no disrespect but to my normal (human) way of thinking – that is just plain dumb. When I am hurting, brokenhearted, beaten and whipped, I do NOT want to think Praise. Just being honest.

But I learned yesterday after trying Dr's, medicines, garlic, ginger, netti pots, liquids, turkey soup, rest... that the ONLY thing that started to work was *PRAISE*. (I am not saying do not go to Dr's, that in this instance God was shaking me to discover who I was relying on).

God told me to share this with you, because the world is starting to shake for many of us and I do not believe God is going to stop shaking the pan just yet.

Just as the above scripture said "the other prisoners were listening to them", people around us will be watching us as their and our world starts shaking. People need to see light in the dark.

Luke 21:9-11 says:
"When you hear of wars and uprisings, do not be frightened. These things must happen first, but the end will not come right away." Then he said to them: "Nation will rise against nation, and kingdom against kingdom. There will be great earthquakes, famines and pestilences in various places, and fearful events and great signs from heaven."

Remember last week the Northern Lights, they pierce the darkness with their glorious light? Well PRAISE unleashes the light. As we go forward this year with God called "eruptions" to our world, personally and around us physically, He wants us to know how to PRAISE HIM and unleash the power and the light around us. He still has hold of the pan, He is not going to let us go, but it may get bumpy.

Are you still singing "This Little Light of Mine?" from last week releasing the light around you – I hope so.

In case you are in the middle of your eruption and you need some Praise Songs, I have given you links to a couple, sit back and raise your hands and sing.

Praise and Release the Power and the Light!

Fairy Tales and Reality

Valentine's Day is a day dedicated to love, often the whole month of February is focused on love, the following story portrays love, truly and completely:

You gather your mail and are surprised as you sift through the endless flyers and bulk "for occupant" mail to see a rather elegant gold metallic envelope in the pile. Your name is written in perfect calligraphic script; curious, you re-check the name. Yes, it is for you. Pleasantly surprised, you expectantly tear and rip it open.

Oh! An invitation.

God has extended an invitation to you to come and meet with Him. He wants to express His love for you and has a gift to give you. Totally overwhelmed, you question this, mulling and swirling dozens of thoughts at one time around in your mind. Who are you to be invited into the presence of the King, yet alone be given a gift? Who are you that you should be noticed?

You wonder if you should go, yet you know that you will. You begin to plan what to wear, something that will make you look...not plain, for that is the way you feel inside: plain, ordinary, nothing special. The outfit will make the difference! And yet, deep down, you know the outfit will not change anything; you will still be the same ordinary person you know you are.

On the day of the event you spend your time primping and fussing until at last, with an exasperated sigh, you conclude there is not much else you can do with yourself; it is as good as it gets, and you go.

You approach the door of the royal palace with tremors in your legs and butterflies in your stomach. The messenger who answers greets you in a fine and royal manner as if he was expecting to see you. He announces that the King is waiting for you and that you are to go right in, as He is expecting you. Startled and looking around you ask if the other guests have arrived, and are even more startled as he tells you that you are to be the only guest.

He leads you into the great room—not just any room, but a radiant room. The elegant, exquisite décor are such that you gasp upon entering such a fine room. You warily glance about the room, sweeping it with your eyes shaking off the feeling like you should not be here.

Then you notice it, the light at the end of the room, a light unlike any other, a warm, comforting light; it seems to beckon you. As you approach the end of the room, you notice the light is being emitted from a figure, a figure seated on a throne; it is the figure of the King.

You approach slowly and then bow down very low to the floor and expectantly wait. Suddenly you feel the presence of a hand upon your shoulder, and you look up, up into eyes that you have never experienced before. You see eyes that portray only warmth, compassion, and something that you cannot imagine that would be there for you: love.

You fluster and start to explain your presence, saying how quite fine it is with you if there was a mix-up in the invitation, for you do not really know why you got invited; you could leave and would not be offended. The radiant face beams down at you. Gently, so very gently, He lifts your head up, cradling your face between both His warm, strong hands.

With a voice oh so tender, He says, "My child, there has been no mix-up. I have been waiting for you. I have longed to meet with you many times; I have longed to share my Kingdom with you. I have sent my messengers out and I would wait by the gate to see if you had accepted my invitations, but always, always, they returned disheartened. I have kept watch over you since the day you were born, in fact, I was at your birth and I even saw you when you were in your mother's womb. Oh, my child, you are more beautiful with each passing day; you have blossomed into a beautiful person. I was so right to give you those eyes. But come, come my child, and talk with me, I so long to hear your voice and hear the longings of your heart. Come."

Hand in hand, you go to a place prepared for just two, and you talk, long, long into the night. He is so easy to talk to; He listens so intently as if you were His only thought in the world. His voice is alive with emotion, and His laugh—oh, His laugh!—it is indescribable.

Then it happens: He gets a look over His face that flashes just for an instant, quick but not quick enough for you not to notice. He tells in a voice so deep and raw with emotion a tale that catches you sharply, and you realize that as He speaks, you are holding your breath. He tells you of an old and ancient enemy that has had spies come into the land to spy and scout out the Kingdom. This enemy has sent a letter, a ransom note, to the King, demanding that in order to preserve peace and not be overtaken in a violent and bloody war that a pact be signed. In sealing the pact, a token must be given to ensure good faith on the King's part.

"The enemy has asked for you, my child, as a sign to seal the pact." As the King is speaking, tears well up in His eyes, and then they overflow, running in streams down His face. "Oh my child, I have searched my

Kingdom over to see what I can do to take away this burden. My heart is heavy within me at the thought of ever losing you or anyone of my kingdom to this enemy. I fear if I do not release you to him he will come in the deep of night and whisk you away. I have been searching for just the right gift to give to seal this pact: a gift that would not only express my love and affection for you and the others in my Kingdom, but one that would also satisfy the enemy.

I know now what that gift must be: a gift that is perfect, unflawed, one that is of the utmost value to me. Not money, nor fame, nor gold or precious gems. You see, my child, these things perish; no, my gift to him will be..."

There is total solemn silence, and He speaks in a slow strained whisper, "...my Son—my own precious Son; the gift will be the Prince."[1]

Do you feel the emotion? The pain?

Could you ever give up your child?

God did not spare His Son for your ransom, for my ransom, for all our ransoms; He gave up His Son, His only Son, to an enemy that He already knew was going to torture and kill Him. He, the King, would not intervene in the procedure, but would have to sit and watch, knowing that in the end this was the only way to defeat that ancient enemy and to save each and every one of those in His kingdom. *

This is no fairy tale, this is reality, my friend, this is how much God loves me, and how much God loves you.

---

[1] *Free to Fly*, Jane Wheeler Chapter 1

"For God so loved the world that He gave His one and only Son that all who believe in Him are saved."
John 3:16

Happy Love Month.

The Loving Thing To Do

This month of love I would like to confront an issue so widespread, it does not have borders; in church, out of the church, financially secure or in poverty, neither skin color nor race, are an issue, it is a racial boundary crosser.

The issue is ***Abuse in the Home.***

Every one of you reading this will have women or children in your orbit that are abused, even if you are not aware of it. In the USA, The Bureau of Justice's National Crime Survey reports that a woman is battered in her home every 15 seconds. (Quoted from: Radio Bible Class, "When Violence Comes Home" Booklet, page 4).

No matter what city or country you are in, there should be a safe place for battered women to flee to. Find out the name and the phone number of your place and have it available to give to a woman who might need it.

I am sure when I talk about abuse, you have a picture in your mind of a battered and bruised woman. Abuse can be emotional as well a physical. Anytime power is exerted over another human being to make them behave in some kind of way, abuse is being done. It can be directed at children, wives and husbands. Yes, husbands can be abused by women as well but in most cases and for this article – we will focus on women and children being the victims.

I have helped many women with this issue, including me so I have a pretty good idea of what I am talking about. I have seen churches ignore this issue, I know women who have been told to just go home and love their husbands. I know women who have been told to go home and be quiet. I have seen churches who bravely take a stand on this issue.

I have also helped women outside of the church, women who have had nowhere to go and express their pain safely.

Abuse is only powerful when it is silent. It is time to break the silence..............

At the beginning of December, I was driving along at 9:30 at night, it was minus 20 out and I drove by a woman standing in her driveway holding a baby. There was "stuff" littered all over the ground around her. I turned around and went back because my gut told me something was very wrong. I got out of my car and went over to her and asked her if she was "all right?" She broke down and shook her head no. I held her and told her it was okay, that I understood. I asked her what I could do as I looked around and saw baby items scattered all over the ground. It was very obvious that she and the baby had been forced out of a car and their belongings had been chucked out all over the ground. This woman had been left with a baby, only a few months old in minus 20-degree weather.

I held the baby and she asked me to take the baby inside while she picked up all the stuff, she apologized to me over and over and over (abused women often apologize for someone else's actions).

Is this a one-time incident? No, even though I do not know these people I can guarantee you that this is not the first time this man has abused this woman. I left my name and directions to my house (very close by) with this woman so that she can come anytime day or night if she needs safety. I did not need to tell her to call 911, she is fully aware of how to do that. She first

[33]

needs to recognize that she is an abuse victim, then she needs to break the silence and the power that abuse holds over her.

This woman was standing in a fourplex situated in a residential neighborhood, houses lined the street. Not one person had come out to offer to help, even when I arrived and stood there with her, not one person ventured out to come and help. This includes her brother in law, who was in the house we were in front of.

People do not wish to be involved and their silence screams out at the victim: 'it must be your fault' and allows the abuser to think it is okay to behave this way.

Abuse is a cycle. Often abuse can escalate into full on violence, sometimes it will be yelling, degrading words or name calling. Abuse can come in any of the following forms:

<u>Being held captive in your home</u> – no vehicle to drive, no way to leave
<u>Not being allowed to have friends or family</u> – isolation
<u>Money, Finances</u> – all controlled by the abuser
<u>Intimidation</u> – verbal or physical
<u>Belittling</u> – an abuser makes it seem like all the abuse is the victim's fault – "if only you were better at..."
<u>Physical</u> – punching, shoving, slapping, choking, sexual advances, rape
<u>Infidelity</u> – spouse has other sexual partners, or sexually abuses the children
<u>Pornography</u>
<u>Murder</u> – is the final stage for an out of control abuser

By the time a woman realizes she is abused she usually has no self-esteem left. She does not feel she is worthy of "saving", she thinks it is probably her fault that he gets so mad or does what he does. If only she tried a little harder. He was so nice before they were married, she can make him get better. Where would she go? How would she support herself?

All of these lies become deeply entrenched into a woman's soul at the hands of an abuser.

What can we as bystanders do?   *Break the silence.*

I remember a phrase that stuck out to me: "I love you too much to let you behave like that." Love is not keeping silent, it is wanting the best for others. When we discipline our children, it is because we love them, we want the best for them. When we speak out on abuse it is because we know there is a better way, we care and it is a loving thing to do.

Support your local women's shelters.

Talk about it! If you suspect abuse in a home – ask.

Let women in the church know that your church will not put up with abuse that it will take a stand and support both the abuser (if possible) and the victim.

Let your church become a safe place for women and children to be, please let them know someone cares. Women need to hear men take a stand against abuse. Women can help women but men need to confront the abuser and ensure safety for the women and children.

Support organizations like Focus on the Family and Radio Bible Class who make huge strides to help families and marriages.

Download or get a copy of the following RBC (Radio Bible Class) pamphlet and read it – several times, so you can know the symptoms of the abuse cycle. Have it available to give to victims that might need to read it. It changed my life.

https://discoveryseries.org/discovery-series/when-violence-comes-home-help-for-victims-of-spouse-abuse/

Stop Hunger Now

I had the opportunity to be part of a Stop Hunger Now event last weekend. I had heard on the radio and in the newspaper that our local Rotary club was looking for 800 volunteers to package some meals. They offered 4 x 2 hours slots that you could pick from, I signed up online, it was super easy to register.

You do not have to be a Rotarian.

I figured I could manage 2 hours to go and see what it was all about. I called my friend and asked if she was interested and off we went.

We are **SO** glad we went, what a very cool and fun event to be part of.

In 2 hours our team of volunteers (adults and children) packaged over 60,000 meals! In total the volunteers for the day packaged 285,000 meals that are heading off to Cambodia. We beat last year's record!

You were assigned to one of the following groups:
1. Funnel station – placing the actual food into bags (1 package can feed 6 people) Each bag contains: Rice, Soy Protein, Dehydrated Vegetables, Vitamin Packet
2. Weighing station – to ensure each bag had the proper amount in it
3. Sealing the bags
4. Boxing – placing 36 bags into each box and taping shut

We were boxers, we got a rhythm going and cannot count how many boxes we filled, but the whole system they have in place is a well-oiled machine. They have obviously done this before, it is very efficient and a lot of fun, complete with a sense of something much bigger than you.

Some of the facts about Stop Hunger Now that I discovered:

Since the launch of STOP HUNGER NOW's meal packaging program in 2005, Rotarians have packaged 20 million+ meals for distribution around the globe. Rotary is a critical link to helping STOP HUNGER NOW meet the United Nations goal of ending world hunger by 2030.

It is immensely fun, a hands-on and rewarding experience for anyone of any age.

Rotary clubs start to recruit volunteers based on the number of meals that it plans to package. It costs approximately 29 cents for each meal that is packaged.

Stop Hunger Now packages and ships meals to feed people in need around the world. The program has engaged millions of Rotary, corporate, student, civic and faith-based volunteers to package meals. Through these efforts, Stop Hunger Now educates thousands of people each year about hunger and inspires them to help end it.

Rotary clubs all over the globe are hosting similar events, look them up and see when there will be one near you, then add your name to the list, you will be glad you did!

The Other 99

Matthew 18:12-14 12
"What do you think? If a man owns a hundred sheep, and one of them wanders away, will he not leave the ninety-nine on the hills and go to look for the one that wandered off? And if he finds it, truly I tell you, he is happier about that one sheep than about the ninety-nine that did not wander off. In the same way your Father in heaven is not willing that any of these little ones should perish." (See also Luke 15:4-7)

I do not know about you but I have often wondered about why God calls Jesus the Shepherd and why He compares us to sheep (not lambs, the cute cuddly babies, but sheep). I did a bit of a comparison chart – interestingly, we have a lot of the same attributes.

➢ Over 1 billion sheep in the world, China has most sheep	➢ Over 7 billion people in the world. China has the most people
➢ Wide range of colors - sheep range from pure white to dark chocolate brown, & spotted	➢ Wide range of colors from pure white to dark chocolate brown
➢ Mature sheep have 32 teeth	➢ Humans have 32 teeth
➢ Sheep are flock animals, inclined to follow the leader	➢ Humans are inclined to group together and follow the leader
➢ Sheep become stressed when separated from flock, closest to related sheep	➢ Humans become stressed when separated from their families, peers – usually closest to their families
➢ Sheep flee from danger	➢ Humans flee from danger
➢ Flock behavior is found in groups of 4 or more.	➢ Humans exhibit flock mentality – in groups of 4

Solitary sheep may not react the same when alone	or more – they may react differently than when alone
➤ Sheep are food orientated – can be led by the food bucket	➤ Humans are food orientated – can be led by food, smorgasbords, pot lucks
➤ Sheep establish a dominance hierarchy	➤ Humans establish a dominance hierarchy
➤ Sheep are quite intelligent, have good memories and are capable of problem solving	➤ Humans are quite intelligent, have good memories and are capable of problem solving
➤ Have been known to self-medicate when ill by eating certain plants	➤ Humans self-medicate on a regular basis
➤ Hygiene can be lacking, smelly, chunks of stuff in wool, matted	➤ Hygiene can be lacking, and smelly and unkempt
➤ Sheep know their shepherds voice	➤ Humans should know their Shepherds voice

In the above scripture in Matthew 18, it tells us that the shepherd left the 99 sheep to go look for the 1 lost one. It seems that that one sheep was of utmost importance to him. Of course the parallel we are supposed to glean from the story is that our Heavenly Shepherd will go off to find that 1 lost person as well. That 1 lost person is too much to lose even if there are 99 left. The verse says "he is happier about that one sheep than about the other 99 that did not wander off."

Those 99 that got left, are the sheep that are content to go along with the status quo. They are not wanderers, they do not have to have a fence, they will stay the course and follow the crowd. They are content to just be, they are comfortable. They did not notice that there was a lost member, they did not go looking, but the shepherd did. Churches can be like this, they are content to keep the status quo, they usually do not go looking for the lost sheep. The 99 are the "stable" church attenders, the tithers, they keep the church going, they do not rock the boat – so why go looking for trouble?

The 1 lost sheep could be the curious one; the hurt one; the smelly unkempt one; the problem in the crowd; the one pushing the limits and breaking the rules, and often labelled as the trouble maker.

To most of us this 1 sheep is the one we roll our eyes at, the one we judge, the one we hope will just stay away because they take a lot of effort and for what? I mean they do not appreciate all the effort you give them, they just keep wandering away.

But I want us to focus on the shepherd's reaction.

The shepherd was not content to lose even 1 sheep. You see even if there was only 1 person on earth, 1 lost, wandering, smelly, needy and unkempt person – Jesus still would have gone to the cross for them. Jesus thinks every single person is worth saving and since we are created in His image, the image of God, not the image of sheep, should that not be our motto as well?

I know for myself, that I often struggle with reaching out to those whom I deem unlovable, the trouble makers or the outcasts, so I am talking to myself here.

Who today is on my/your wandering sheep list? Are

you/I willing to break away from our flock, our comfort zone and go looking for them as Jesus did, or are we content to stay in our field and stick with our flock?

A Families Journey in Aging Part 1

I feel it is time to write a bit about my family's journey - the journey of aging.

I write this not as an expert in any way but as a friend who wants to come along side and perhaps, help you see the things that maybe we missed, the questions you might be able to ask, the steps you should take, before it is too late.

I am talking about Alzheimer's and Dementia.
Stats:
16,000 Canadians under age 65 live with dementia
25,000 is the number of new cases of dementia diagnosed every year
564,000 the number of current Canadians currently living with dementia
1.1 million the number of Canadians affected directly or indirectly by the disease
*Dementia numbers in Canada | Alzheimer Society of Canada

Alzheimer's is an irreversible disease that destroys brain cells, causing thinking ability and memory to deteriorate. It is not a normal part of aging. It is a type of Dementia.

Dementia is a term for a whole set of symptoms including impaired thinking and memory. It can affect communication and interfere with doing daily activities. There are different kinds of Dementia depending on where the damage is in the brain. Alzheimer's is one kind of Dementia.

A long time ago, 20+ years ago we noticed my Moms memory was not what it used to be, at the time we did not know what to do, if anything, because it was not so

[43]

bad that Mom could not function. It was annoying when she could not remember, or failed to show up for an event, but Dad took on the task of remembering for her. We realized later that Dad covered for Mom a lot probably because he did not want to be embarrassed or have Mom embarrassed. I am not quite sure when we realized that Mom had Alzheimer's and maybe we never spoke the word until after the Dr. said it, but we sure thought about it.

Hindsight is always so much brighter. We now know that Mom and Dad's neighbors knew there was stuff going on that caused them concern, but no one ever talked to us, the kids (although we were now adults).

Although one or more of us was seeing Mom/Dad regularly we did not live there, with them. A relative coming and going weekly or bi-weekly would not notice the little things that just did not add up, or would slough them off as "weird" but nothing to worry about. Neighbors usually have the benefit of seeing people every day or so and when things do not add up, they are the first in line to spot it. I wish someone had come and talked to us. If you have some questions about your parents - ask the neighbors if they have noticed any changes.

In the fall of 2010, now looking back, we saw some changes in Dad that we could not figure out, so we ignored it for the first part. Then came December 18, 2010, when our lives would forever change.

I remember the phone call from my sister, "Dad called Rob (my brother) this morning to let him know that mom did not come home last night."

My brain swirled into panic mode since Mom has Alzheimer's - how long was she out there? Where was she? Did they find her?

My sister continued, "Rob called the police, they and the fire department came and when they knocked on the door, Dad answered and Mom was standing there right beside him. He told the police that he had not seen his wife all night and she had not come home."

They took my Dad to the hospital.

For us it was the start of what we call - "The crazy years".

Dad probably never recognized mom again and went on to look for her for the next three years. He overnight had lost sight of her. He was often looking for his mother or his wife. He regressed back to a very young age, probably late teens, early twenties - just home from the Korean war.

Please read more of our journey in next week's blog...

A Families Journey in Aging Part 2

For us it was the start of what we call - "The crazy years".

Dad probably never recognized mom again and went on to look for her for the next three years. He overnight had lost sight of her. He was often looking for his mother or his wife. He regressed back to a very young age, probably late teens, early twenties - just home from the Korean war.

Since Dad was Mom's caregiver , we now suddenly had 2 broken parents to look after. We took them to the Doctor and he diagnosed Mom with Alzheimer's and Dad with Dementia. He spoke to them that it was time to look at moving into an Assisted Living facility.

Mom and Dad seemed stunned at the diagnosis. All 5 of us were there and us 3 kids were so thankful that the Doctor had done the "hard" talk to our parents. At least so we thought, *we had no idea* we would be repeating this story hundreds of times more.

We took them home that day and discussed moving options and places and made a plan to go look at some places. Low and behold when we went to get them the next day they could not remember the Doctors visit or the fact that they had anything wrong with them and were indignant that we would even think of moving them to another place.

Now it was our turn to be stunned and we were not sure what to do. We finally got them to look at a couple of options for "down the road", but always the place was not good enough and down the road was a long ways off to them.

Then we ran into the fact that most Assisted Living places do NOT take people with Dementia or Alzheimer's: that really limited our options and our hopes slumped. We visited a couple of places that take Dementia only patients and more often than not my sister and I would leave crying and distressed at the thought of ever putting our parents in there.

We, the kids, went to Mom & Dad's lawyer and asked about a Power of Attorney - Mom and Dad had done one up approximately 1 1/2 years prior- thank goodness (please ensure you do this for your children and your own sake). They also had a living will and had a Last Will and Testament on file; after being diagnosed with Dementia you cannot make or change a Will.

However, Mom and Dad's Power of Attorney said that we had to have 2 Doctor's give the same diagnosis to become effective. How do you get your parents to another Doctor they do not know, when they do not even think there is something wrong with them, never mind tell them you think they have Dementia? It was a battle, but we got it done. I understand the concept of getting 2 doctors diagnosis, but with Dementia, everything becomes a battle since they are not thinking clearly.

Two Doctors with the same diagnosis, for us, solidified that Mom and Dad were not going to "snap out of it" or "get better." We knew we had to do something about them living on their own but we did not know what or how, especially when our parents were arguing with us each step of the way.

A few incidents pushed us into action:
1) I discovered a hole in the enamel in the top of their stove, when I had moved a hot pad. I asked Dad what had happened. He came over and replaced the hot pad

and whispered, "Your mom left the frying pan on one day and walked away. Just leave the hot pad on there and no one will see it." I stared at the stove top and wondered just how hot that stove had to get to actually melt the enamel.

2) We found out that mom and dad had flooded the townhouse underneath them since mom had used the hose on the laundry tub to help the washing machine fill up faster and walked away. This caused the "flood" that caused $12,000 in damage to the downstairs neighbors, who were not so very happy about this.

3) My brother was getting phone calls from residents in the complex that Mom and Dad lived in asking if indeed Mom and passed away. Dad was telling everyone that Mom had died (he could not recognize her).

Mom and Dad were still adamant that they would not move. Being creative we tried to hire nurses, aides, companions, to come and be at the house for a good portion of the day to look out for Mom and Dad. They either fired them or would not let them into the house because they had no idea who they were or why they would be needed since everything was "fine".

We would have family meetings, explain how things were and get them to agree to move, only to have them cancel the next day or the day after. They said they had no idea of what we were talking about and insisted they had certainly not been to a Doctor or had any Doctor tell them they had Alzheimer's. We got them signed into a place, which was lovely, arranged a moving company to come, only to have Dad tell them in no uncertain terms that he was not moving and he had no idea what they were talking about. This happened more than several times.

One day, 3 or 4 months later, we just showed up, us 3 kids, and a moving truck and we sent them out on an errand and packed up the house. It felt horrible, it caused us such guilt, but we did not know what else to do. I remember that on the day we were packing them up, neighbors then came and told us they were glad we were taking care of Mom and Dad, they had noticed they had not been "right" lately and their driving scared them. I sigh now, just thinking if they had only come and told us before it got so bad.

Now I would like to tell you that it went well and that my parents were keen on moving. It was not like that. We placed them into an amazing Assisted Living place, much like a 5 star hotel, truly I would love to live there.

We spent the next year fighting with Mom and Dad and kept having to cancel moving companies when they showed up because Dad had called them to move home. They would drive around trying to get home (they were an hour from their old house). Dad was never good with directions and Mom with Alzheimer's could not remember where they were trying to get to. Sometimes the staff at the home would watch Mom and Dad drive around the parking garage trying to find their way out for extended periods of time.

Dad lost his Driver's License during this time, he failed his Driver's exam. He drove anyways, since he could not remember that he could not drive. Mom also drove sometimes, and that was even scarier, because she had no idea where she was going, she could not remember. She ended up losing her Driver's license as well. We finally took the car away because they kept driving without licenses.

This was our 3 years of crazy and or as we refer to them, the "hell" years. Sometimes we felt like we were the "crazy" ones. We laughed, cried and guilted ourselves until it hurt, sometimes we fought each other because the pain we felt had to come out in some kind of fashion or eat us alive.

I am only sharing the "tip" of the iceberg, there are so many events, stories, emotions that go with this complete story.

Please Read Part 3 - 'signs and symptoms to watch for' - next week...

A Families Journey in Aging Part 3

This was our 3 years of crazy and or as we refer to them, the "hell" years. Sometimes we felt like we were the "crazy" ones. We laughed, cried and guilted ourselves til it hurt, sometimes we fought each other because the pain we felt had to come out in some kind of fashion or eat us alive.

I wish I had known then what I know now, what to watch for, how to intervene earlier rather than later. If you notice behavior changes that do not make sense, memory loss that seems more than just "aging" do NOT ignore it, for your sake and theirs.

The very first rule you should know is: **DO NOT TAKE ANY THING THEY SAY OR DO PERSONALLY; YOU HAVE TO DISASSOCIATE EMOTIONALLY FROM THEM - they have a disease.**

(Really tough to do with parents and even more so with a spouse)

We probably did this too late because we did not know what we were doing or dealing with, we had no support as caregivers except each other. We found ourselves saying over and over "that is not my mother or that is not my Dad". They might look and sound like them, but it is the disease talking.

Find a support group for yourself , the caregiver, even if they are in a care home, <u>so very important</u>! Get informed and find other people going through the same journey, you will need to talk it out, cry it out and find some ways to laugh.

Things we did that made it easier:

- Made a memory book - photo album, important pictures, places, announcements going right back to the persons childhood if possible.
- We also wrote out their history for the care home so that they could also have "memories" to share with them.

As a person progresses into stage 3 and 4 of Dementia or Alzheimer's, the only pictures they might remember is their own childhood. My mom now does not know who her grandchildren are and often at her stage 4, she forgets us, her own children.

When a person is diagnosed with Alzheimer's or Dementia, their family physician does have to report it to the motor vehicles office. We breathed a sigh of relief that we would not have to face taking the car or trying to get the Driver's licenses. **WRONG.**

Government offices are not notably fast acting. Dad finally had to go for a driving test, but it was 5-6 months after the diagnosis. He failed the driving test but continued to drive because he forgot. Mom's driver's exam was not schedule for 8-9 months after the diagnosis and she ended up failing because she kept forgetting to go for the exam. She continued to drive because she had an expired license in her wallet that told her she could still drive (her mind could not compute the dates, she just needed to see the license).

We as a family had to take the car away, it just disappeared one day; if you think my folks were "happy" about it - think again. More often than not it will be the family having to make this decision for the safety of the person and others on the road.

The list to get older patients into homes is long and the wait is tedious. We found out that they place people into care homes "individually" - not in couples.

We took it upon ourselves and had the resources to get my parents into Assisted Living together. Getting them into total care was another story, it was done individually. Most of the time you are usually dealing with one spouse with Dementia, not both, as in our case. By the time the person goes into a home, it is usually a relief for the caregiving spouse who has been carrying the load probably for a while.

We were told that if one of our parents went into the hospital (before we got them into a facility) to refuse to take them home, that way they had to be placed by the government into a facility faster. You do not get to decide which facility but at least it is full time care.

My niece is now a nurse (we could have used her back then) she gave me a very informative online brochure that lists options that **_ALL_** people need to consider as they age. The forms are for the Province of BC but they certainly can be used as a template for you to make decisions by. She also informed me that in this age of "step families", step parents and step children, that unless it is written down, even a family friend can have a say about medical decisions over a step-child.

Link to "My Voice" Brochure:
http://www.health.gov.bc.ca/library/publications/year/2013/MyVoice-AdvanceCarePlanningGuide.pdf

There is a cylce of events that take place in Dementia and Alzheimer's. It goes from memory loss, to paranoia, where they do not trust anyone, they accuse people of stealing their things often because they have misplaced them, including family. There can be a stage of anger that can range from mild to severe; loss of inhibitions (my friend's grandma used to take her clothes off and run around).

Here are 10 symptoms to watch for from the Alzheimer's Society of Canada:

1. Memory loss affecting day-to-day abilities – forgetting things often or struggling to retain new information.

Regular aging will have memory loss but with Dementia type memory loss, you cannot "recall" what it was you were trying to remember. One of the tests that they gave my parents was a series of questions asking what day of the week is it, what is the date today, what is the month, even what year is it, how old are you? Can you remember what you had for lunch today or breakfast?

2. Difficulty performing familiar tasks – forgetting how to do something you have been doing your whole life, such as preparing a meal or getting dressed.

We noticed Dad had lost the ability to do some of the things he had done for years, but we put it down to "aging".

3. Problems with language – forgetting words or substituting words that don't fit the context.

Dad's communication was what we called "weird" occasionally. He could not remember the right word or struggled to find a word which is not something he had ever done, again we thought it was normal "aging".

4. Disorientation in time and space – not knowing what day of the week it is or getting lost in a familiar place.

This was an interesting one: Dad could not get "time" correct. One day I found him sitting in the hallway on his suitcase at 4 in the morning, I asked what he was doing and he said he did not want to miss his plane, he was six hours early. I shrugged it off cause I did not know what to think. Banks and some businesses told us that Dad had been in several times in a day and they were not sure for what; they did not tell us until after we had put them into the Assisted Living.

5. Impaired judgment – not recognizing a medical problem that needs attention or wearing light clothing on a cold day.

Or leaving a hot item on the stove and walking away or filling the washing machine with a hose and walking away.

6. Problems with abstract thinking – not understanding what numbers signify on a calculator, for example, or how they're used.

Dad was a business man and numbers were his "thing". Imagine how shocked my brother was one day when Dad wrote out a "cheque" on a paper napkin and handed it to him. We could not believe Dad could not get "numbers" - simple addition seemed abstract to him. He loved Suduko but we realized now, that early on in the disease, he could not play any longer - again we did not know it was a sign of Dementia.

7. Misplacing things – putting things in strange places, like an iron in the freezer or a wristwatch in the sugar bowl.

We found things in the strangest places when we moved our parents. We came across 20+ boxes of toothpaste, and overabundance of toilet paper and kleenex (Mom forgot she had bought things).

8. Changes in mood and behavior – exhibiting severe mood swings from being easy-going to quick-tempered.

9. Changes in personality – behaving out of character such as feeling paranoid or threatened.

Mom and Dad often felt paranoid and threatened because they did not understand what was going on.

10. Loss of initiative – losing interest in friends, family and favorite activities, they isolate and people withdraw because they do not know how to relate to them.

Our journey would not have been easy even if we had gotten an earlier diagnosis but it would have been "easy-ier". The journey into Dementia is not one any of us wish to travel but the high incidence of it today, assures me that some us will in fact have to travel the same path with a parent or a spouse or perhaps even ourselves.

The key to recognizing some of the symptoms early is important. Working with your aging loved ones while they can recognize some of the signs and make more coherent decisions early on, will in the long run make your journey not quite so rocky as ours.

One of the key things we found was "crucial" was having some facts written out, photocopied and "stashed" in various places at their house or care home. At the beginning we had the Dr's visit date and diagnosis, along with a photocopied Dr. letter, and a brief synopsis of events (mom flooding the downstairs, leaving the stove on...). This letter where they could read what had happened by fact, (not argument), they were then more open to listening. Or if they phoned one of us and could not figure out what was happening, we could say go look in such and such there should be a letter there, read it, I will wait. As the disease progressed I would update the letter every few months and finally got Mom to write the letter in her own handwriting after Dad passed away. She would recognize her own writing and she knew she could trust herself and that no one was lying to her. Often she would tear the letter up but we always had a good supply of copies on hand (and one at the nurse's station).

Please ensure for the sake of your children that you take action to have a Power of Attorney in Place, A Living Will. This way your loved ones will know your wishes if you are not able to communicate them coherently, and an updated Last Will and Testament. Take the time to list your bank accounts, investments and insurance policies and have them attached to your Last Will and Testament. (My Dad loved to do a lot of banking in his head, not so easy for others to figure it out later).

My Dad passed away March 2013 with severe Dementia in the end he could not communicate or do daily functions.

Mom is still in a Care Home with stage 4 Alzheimer's. Our journey still continues.....

Whistle While You Work

I was at a prayer meeting a while ago and we were talking about life and I found myself complaining about how hard it had been in our marriage lately, it had not been a good week.

One fellow responded by telling me about putting the hardwood down on the floor of his house.

I know, how helpful - right?

The house had been built with two different kinds of flooring so they wanted to put hardwood through the whole house. Most of the house was easy to do but the dining room had been nailed down and he was having a rough time getting it off, so he hired a professional floor guy.

He decided that if he helped the fellow, the job would go much faster but it turned out it did not work that way. For some reason a lot of nails had been put into the old floor and it turned out it was a matter of brute strength and scraping and pulling nails. They both had thought it would be a couple hour job but it took both of them a full day. My friend was experiencing the aches and pains of a weekend reno warrior by the end of the day and he marveled at the professional guy who was whistling the whole time.

Finally not able to hold it in any longer my friend said, "Wow this is a lot harder than I thought it would be."

The professional agreed with him adding, "This was the hardest floor I have ever had to remove."

Incredulous my friend said, "Well I would never have known that, you were whistling and cheerful the whole time. My body is aching and I wanted to give up hours ago."

The professional floor guy said, "Sometimes God gives us really hard jobs along with the easy ones, and I have learned you have to take the good with the bad jobs."

Well I got the analogy: floors, life, marriage, kids, work, whatever it is – it is not guaranteed to be easy but it can be. Sometimes brute strength and determination are needed – but do I take the good with the bad? Have I learned to whistle while I work in both the good and the bad phases? Or do I sit and complain when I do not like it?

Hmmmmmmmm...

Our Youth Pastor gave the sermon and he only spoke maybe 5-7 minutes but what he said was a profound.

"When can God stop having to prove to you that He is God and just be God."

This has gone around and around in my brain since then and I have tried to put it into practice. What I have changed is not asking God to answer my prayers "specifically". What I mean is that I when I pray I now assume that God is God and He will answer it, instead of me telling Him what I want Him to do. For me when I was being "specific" I was actually telling God what to do, me taking over.

Do you know what I have found?

He has shown up more now than for a long time.

What has happened is that I have let God be God, not me trying to get Him to prove He is God or me telling Him what to do.

I actually find this approach freeing, and that can cause me to whistle while I work – I live my life knowing God is going to show up and He does!

Expectations and Expectancy

I probably am going to be the biggest receiver of this blog because it is hitting me very personally.

The words **Expectations and Expectancy**. God has been speaking to me about these for a while. My first teaching at Aglow a year ago was on *Expectations* and here I am still studying it.

There is a huge difference in the two words. I admit I tend to look to God with *Expectations*, well actually I tend to look around me at my family, friends, employer, pretty much everything with *Expectations*.

Expectations can either make or break you. We enter into every situation, relationship or event in life with *expectations*.

Definition of Expectation: Noun (person, place of thing, a stationary word), a strong belief that something will happen or be the case in the future. Synonyms: suppose, assume, presume, conjecture, surmise, calculate, predict... nothing about these words gives us the feeling that an *expectation* is 100% guaranteed.

When we or others do not live up to our *expectations* we get disillusioned. *Expectations* are a form of control, we feel we have the "right" to expect people to act a certain way and heaven help them if they do not! Our spouses, our children, our friends, our pastors, our God...

Looking at the word disillusioned, take off the prefix – 'dis' and we get the word 'illusion'. What exactly is an illusion? Synonyms: false appearance, false belief, daydream, hocus-pocus, make-believe, mirage.

Our *expectations* are a delusion on our part, a daydream, or make-believe. We are setting ourselves and others up for absolute failure if we put our *expectations* in people or even in God.

It is basically an illusion – or magic, if you will. To live this way is a short path to disillusionment and often heart break. The only person you can try to control is yourself.

Definition of Expectancy - Verb (action word, moving)- an attitude of anticipation, eagerness, wonder

I have an *expectancy* that God is going to do something. In an *expectation* I believe God had better do something and it better look like what I think it should.

In *expectancy,* God is going to do something and I wonder what His is up to or wonder how He will do it but I am confident that He is going to show up, I just do not know how.

The Book of Job in the Bible, at first glance we *expect* that it is a horrible story about a poor guy who loses everything. We cannot figure it out, we, as well as back then, *expect* that if we "obey" God, God will Bless us. Job obeyed and it does not look like Job got blessed. As a matter of fact Job had a few friends that stayed with him through his ordeal reminding Job continuously that it was *expected* that if Job had obeyed God, Job would have been Blessed. Job was not blessed so they *expected* and told Job over and over that Job had to have disobeyed. At the end of the story we find out that Job did not disobey. Way to break an *expectation*!

The Book of Job is actually not about Job. Phillip Yancy first opened my eyes to this in his book "The Bible Jesus Read" that the Book of Job is a story about God. God and satan have a "contest" and God placed His *expectancy* on Job to prove to satan that God is worth loving no matter what. Job came through.

It is my favorite book of the Bible maybe because I relate to a lot of Jobs pain. But when I mention Job to most folks, they focus on Job, they do not see the bigger picture, the behind the scene struggle between God and satan. That struggle is the ultimate point of the whole book: God is worth loving regardless if you are being blessed or feel cursed.

Most of us have had some kind of "Job" trials come into our life at some time or other. If we become bogged down by life's problems and face them with *expectations* – we will surely be disillusioned. We put our *expectation* on God and even pray He will meet our *expectations*. We are trying to be in control of the situation this way. Us in control – not God.

If we face life with an *"expectancy"* – knowing that God is going to work things out – it becomes more of anticipation and wondering what is going to happen and how God will work things out. Oh there will still be problems and struggles, but we face them not with discouragement, but with *expectancy*...

This was reinforced to me the other night when I watched the final session of our Aglow, *Game Changer* video (a really awesome study). The speaker Graham Cooke does a mini skit – showing how to handle a crisis with *expectancy*.

"Hey John, it's Graham.....I am calling because something amazing happened today. Yeah, I got this problem. Hey, it looks really big. Yeah, I am super excited – like I am beside myself.... Yeah, it is like, I am looking and I am thinking, if the problem is that big, how much bigger is the promise and then how much bigger than the promise is the provision? Yeah, it is amazing; I am so super excited I wanted you to know. So how you doing anyway? You do not have a problem? One is bound to come, do not fret. Hey listen, do you want to share this one with me? No it would be cool. Come over and we will kind of work on it together and whatever blessing you get, that will be great. Yeah...."

Do we believe God is bigger than our problems?

Do we believe that God is not wringing His hands over our problems? That He has a solution, even if our eyes cannot see a way out or around our problem.

The God who created the universe, who formed something out of nothing can handle it.

This is what I am in the process of learning – how to hold on with a much looser grip, a grip that says...

"Hey I have a problem. No it's exciting, it's really big. Yeah, I am pumped to see what God is going to do with it and how He is going to show up, it is going to be amazing, really amazing..."

Me

I have felt for a long time that I am on a journey, not sure *how* I am going to get there but very confident of the destination.

I seem to be a person without deep roots. Now some of you who have known me for 5, 10 or even 20 years might question that. I have wondered about it too, I know that for me, my kids are my deepest roots.

As I review my life I have seen a pattern. At first the intervals were longer, but then my children were small. My heart is for my children and having stability was important for me to gift to them.

But as they grew and matured, the intervals or the timing of my moving from place to place was shortening. I am not talking about just "physical" moves which I know I did a lot for a while. More I mean the moving in and out of people's lives; the ebb and tide of people.

I got to calling me a 'fixer' in many of the job positions that I took on. God would move me into a job opportunity that needed some help. I would be in the position for a "relatively" short period of time and then move on to the next.

Now as I reflect, it was not just the jobs but also people's lives that I was able to flow in and out of. Sometimes I would not understand the need to move on and rant to God about why it was not right or fair and let Him know I did not like it; sometimes I knew I was there in a crisis time – more like a stretcher bearer. Those people who you come across when the accident or trauma happens, fresh wounds, incredible pain, and spiritual chaos. Just like a paramedic – they come in and assess you, bandage you, put salve on the wounds, give you something for the pain and get you to help. They do not stay for the long term, they get you stable and ensure you are in capable, safe hands and they move on.

If you have ever heard of Mark Gungor's Flag Pages – it is a method of figuring out your strengths and characteristics that govern your life. My overwhelming priority according to my Flag Page assessment is "loyalty". I do wholeheartedly agree with that.

I recently had a meltdown of epic proportions and overwhelming guilt over the fact that I not been able to walk with each person who has been in my life long term to this day. I felt I had let people down, let myself down and had let God down (the loyalty factor).
I still bear their wounds, now scars in my soul to this day. Each person became so special to me, so endeared to me, each claiming a piece of my heart. I still pray for them to this day.

God in His mercy sent me a sweet message in several parts which He intricately wove together until it made sense.
1. Years ago in over a 6 month period – prophetically 3 people came up to me (1 did not even know me) and told me that I was called to be a "teacher". These were some incredible "wow" moments for me, not sure I truly believed it at the time.
2. God sent me to a high school. I learned first-hand that teachers cannot humanly remember every child they taught. Oh some are unforgettable but their job was to use the time they had together to instruct, guide, and love them for the time they had.
3. A friend prophetically told me that I am given tasks by God "by assignment" – hence the no deep roots. This spoke profoundly to my soul, it tied all

my jobs and ebb and flow of people together into a fragrant offering that I could lift up to God and say – 'Lord I did what I could... you take them from here'. It was a protection that I had not seen, as I a mere human do not have the resources that people need – God does. This took me a while to figure out, but I came to realize, that if I loved people where they were at – people would be left knowing that I loved them but more than that, knowing that God loved them profoundly more.

As I was walking onto another plane today, I heard people talking about "home" and as much as I have a house, I am not sure where "home" actually is for me.

I heard God whisper to my heart that I may never have deep roots that I have more assignments to come. It was a bittersweet message because as I yearn for a solid footing physically, it was sweet because I have more people to meet.

I have found my life to be frustrating, exciting, fun, excruciating, painful, full, all with a definite ebb and flow, but assuredly **never dull and boring** – all because I have learned to take my marching orders from God.

Work Yourself Out of A Job

I find I still get caught up in the stress of "doing". I think satan loves it when we are too busy because then we have no time to fit God into our schedules.

One of the statements in the Aglow Bible study Game Changers I have been doing says: *"Rest is a weapon."* Now think about that, 'rest is a weapon'.

Oswald Chambers (my favorite devotional) says, *"The greatest competitor of true devotion to Jesus is the service we do for Him. It is easier to serve than pour out our lives completely for Him."* My Utmost for His Highest, January 18

"It is easier to serve" basically it is me calling the shots, I will serve where and when I want to rather than giving my life wholly to God and saying "use me wherever you wish...." thus letting God call the shots. That can be too scary because what if He asks me to do...............you fill in the blank.....that horrible thing I do not ever want to do?

God has been asking me - personally to be *"all in"*.

To me, in my old nature, I think this means ramping up to do more "stuff", but I realize that is NOT what God means at all with the term: *all in. God wants me to pour out my life to Him*, not do more stuff. What is the difference?

I find that when I do more stuff I tend to forget Him in the busyness that follows.

In my previous Manager roles, God had to get me to face some misconceptions about Managers/Leaders and these myths can be applied to families as well.

Myth 1: As a leader it is my job to help all the people all the time.

Moses thought the same thing:

"The next day Moses took his seat to serve as judge for the people, and they stood around him from morning till evening. When his father-in-law saw all that Moses was doing for the people, he said, "What is this you are doing for the people? Why do you alone sit as judge, while all these people stand around you from morning till evening?"

Moses answered him, "Because the people come to me to seek God's will. Whenever they have a dispute, it is brought to me, and I decide between the parties and inform them of God's decrees and instructions."

Moses' father-in-law replied, "What you are doing is not good. You and these people who come to you will only wear yourselves out. The work is too heavy for you; you cannot handle it alone. Listen now to me and I will give you some advice, and may God be with you." Exodus 18:13-19

Answer: You cannot handle it alone – **you need help, get some.**

Myth 2: I cannot get my fellow helpers, workers, staff, kids to do part of my job.

Why not? Chances are some of them will do a better job than you anyways and if they do not, practice makes perfect! **Train** them and then **Empower** them to try it out! Give your employees purpose not rules.

Notice that you have to "**Train them**". I learned this after years of not doing it; you **have to** schedule into your calendar "**Training**". It seems like one more thing to do BUT in the end it is worth it. We think employees

[69]

come knowing what they should do, they do not and neither do children. If you want another person to know something, then teach and model it.

When I first started working I worked for the government and at one of the training seminars I attended they gave us this story. (Disclaimer: I might not have all the details correct but this is how I remember it).

Disney has one of the best **training** programs in the history of companies. They listen to their employees, they hire for attitude not skill, they *teach and empower* their employees to make decisions and do not chastise them for doing so.

Story: A young newlywed couple booked their wedding night at the Disneyland Hotel. They checked in and got their key and starry eyed, went up to the Honeymoon suite oblivious to all others around them.

He put the key into the door, pushed it open and turned to lift up his bride and carry her across the threshold only to hear the screams coming out of the room from another couple happily enjoying the Honeymoon suite already.

Stunned he put his bride down, frantically grabbed for the door to close it and horrified they rushed back to the elevator.

Downstairs at the front desk a young girl answered the 'in house' phone and got a verbal chewing out from the couple currently occupying the room, with the statement that they would be down shortly to check out because their wedding night had been wrecked forever by the hotel.

The front desk girl quickly got hold of the night manager and he quickly on the spot made the decision to get the girl to take care of the newlyweds in the elevator as they would be coming off the elevator any second and he himself would take the couple upstairs since they also would be storming down shortly.

This night manager – had been *taught and empowered* to handle the situation and he trusted his staff member in turn, to make some on the spot decisions to remedy this situation with the newlyweds.

The elevator opened and out came the fuming couple towards the front desk. The girl took the couple aside and profusely began apologizing for the mix up in rooms and told them she understood their anger. She would find them another hotel if they wished but she was willing to put them up in another room in the hotel, guaranteed to be unused and offered that the hotel would be willing to pay for their entire stay including meals for their honeymoon if they wished. They stayed.

The night manager went up to the room to the couple who had been walked in on and offered them his most sincere apologies. He told them he understood their anger and embarrassment and that nothing could erase that but if they would allow him, the hotel would like to try to make it up to them by covering the cost of their entire stay and meals Plus the hotel would honored if they came back every year on their anniversary as guests of the hotel.

This couple ended up staying for their honeymoon and this couple kept coming back to the hotel every year for 50+ years on their anniversary.

If these staff members had not been given the skills and the empowerment by the management to make decisions and knew that the ramifications of their decisions would not be questioned by the management, this story could have had a less than happy ending. The staff would be fired for the initial room mix-up and for "giving away" rooms and meals, or the hotel guests would have found other hotels, and the bad press of the incident would have run rampant.

Instead, this story has been shared in, too many to count, leadership seminars as the perfect example of how to empower your employees to make decisions on their own. Disney came out the true winner of these stories and *all ended up Happily Ever After.*

Myth 3: As a leader I cannot take time off.

Why not? God rested on the 7th day, why should you not be able to?
Rest is a weapon: a person who is rested and refreshed will actually do more work than a person who is hanging in there 24/7 and is frantically trying to get it all done. Without rest you do not work productively (oh boy do I know this one!)

Myth 4: As a leader I have to have all the answers.

Who are you – God?
Do not assume like I often did, that you are the smartest person in the building! It is a proven fact that workers, or family members when asked and brought into the decision making stages of a job or project, take on ownership and will work more effectively, so let them!

Myth 5: As a leader I have to be available 24/7 to my staff or family.

Why?

Turn off your phone, do not check your emails continuously, be present where you are at. If there is a problem, empower your staff/family to solve it without you. Lead by example, and take care of yourself, your staff will follow suit and will rise to the challenge you give them.

Illustration: when the little masks in the plane drop down in front of you, what does the stewardess say to do? Please put your own mask on before you go to help others. You will not be able to help others without air, or strength, or wisdom because you too tired to function.

I was encouraged as a leader to find out what I was **not** good at and eliminate it from my job description, giving it away to someone else. This is brutal if you are a controller. **Consider this:** it is probably safe to assume that anyone who works with you already knows you are not good at anyways (just saying).

Summary: Understand Rest is a Weapon; Realize you do not have all the answers; Take a break from work and be present at home or wherever you are; Recognize that you are not the smartest person in the organization; Work yourself out of a job.

You are off to a great start!
The role of a true manager, leader, parent, is to train others up to take your place, or in the instance of kids – train them up to survive without you – work yourself out of a job!

Jesus trained His disciples to carry on the work without Him, and so must you.

All in all it is a win/win situation.

Perspective From the Library

Oh my, the time has flown by from September to now in the Library. If anyone had told me last summer that I was going to be a Librarian at a High School I would not have believed them!

The students have endeared themselves to my heart and I will miss them if I continue on my way. I am not sure what is going to happen, God has not given me a clue what the fall holds for me either.

We have our Grad ceremonies in 3 weeks and a week past that Awards night and then final exams.

I realize now that the main goal in the Library is for me to be a "mom", love and guide more than anything. I am the only person who can take cell phones away because they are writing a test (I do enjoy this part maybe too much, watching them squirm when their phone vibrates and not being able to jump up and see who is texting.)

There is a "language" rule in the library and I enforce it! Love it when one of my regulars lets a word slip and I look up and say "Language!" and she shoots back - that was not a swear word, it was *'butterfly'* in "Afrikaans". (she is from South Africa).
Um hmm....

I will miss the hugs that warm my soul and the stories that entertain and make me giggle:

One of my regular Library attenders was telling me that out on their farm there is a dead moose carcass. The neighbor had spotted bears in the area and her family had spotted a group of coyotes coming in close. She said that she was feeling afraid to go for a walk on the property with animals coming in so close.

The authorities had been called, had come but the moose was too big for the winch they brought, so there it sat.

She told me that when she had gone for a walk one day she had looked for the pepper spray but could not find it so she took the Lysol instead.

This made my head whip around. "The Lysol?" I asked her.

Yes the Lysol. I commented that it would be a clean bear then, very sanitized.

She replied that she figured the bear would get distracted by the lemony scent giving her a chance to escape.

Bless her heart – she was serious! I told her that possibly she should find something different.

My heart goes out to the students who struggle to be "students", learning does not come easy to them but they try and give it their all just get a passing grade. Then there are those elite learners who dominate the "honor roll". Then there are the loners who seem to have no friends and come to the library to escape the crowded hallways.

We had a writing contest in the library and wow can some of these students write! It blows my mind the imagination and degree of thought some of them give to their stories.

I have learned that a good deal of the students have a lack of hope and meaning in their lives. I have heard teachers say that this is a different generation and they do not know what to do with them. I have had teachers come in to the Library and tell me kids are playing games on their phones and one girl is painting her nails in their class, and this teacher was complaining because the kids are not listening.

I have a new appreciation for our teachers, they work hard and put up with a lot. In many students there is a lack of commitment or work ethic. They think nothing of skipping class or taking days off, they know they will pass and you know they probably will. There is no failing these days. The only time this will become a problem is when a College or University bases entrance requirements on their marks. Many will come back for upgrading and re-do's or drift off into life instead of continuing their education.

I read today a letter from one of our "honors" kids, he wrote it to a scholarship committee and he asked me to proof it. In Ireland and in Germany they had a course load of 9 major courses per semester, no electives, core courses, including 3 different languages. I was listening at the same time to some of our "Canada" students complain because they had 3 courses (and 1 spare) and it was too hard! It was enlightening to see the difference in expectations in the different countries and the value difference the 2 cultures have on education.

At a staff meeting a couple weeks ago we were told they are introducing a new course for Grade 10's. They have realized that students do not have keyboarding skills anymore. Texting does not cut it apparently in the essay and keyboard department so we will be playing catch-up.

I was introduced to a 15 minute video clip that describes this generation, affectionately named "millennials" even though many "millennials" hate being labeled thus. Simon Sinek was able to put into words what parents, teachers, employers and students are feeling, the tug of war on both sides. He gives some remedies that must take place to help these young people mature into the next generation. It is well worth the 15 minutes so please take the time to watch it.

Link to Simons video interview:

https://www.youtube.com/watch?v=hER0Qp6QJNU

Crapertunities

I am a logophile, a lover of words.

I have a 'word a day' calendar in the Library and am always excited to experience the new word of the day.

Last week there were some fun ones:
Dreck – rubbish or trash
Fleer – to laugh imprudently or jeeringly
Bushwa is my favorite! - rubbish or nonsense

I admit that sometimes I make up words just because they sound cool! For years I said "ped-is-train-ians" instead of "ped-es-trians" – because it was so much better sounding.

I was explaining to someone that right now in my circle of life, I, myself, seem to be "okay" but I am surrounded by piles of "doo-doo", you know that gross, icky, smelly stuff, often called crap. It seems that whatever direction I am about to step in, I am going to step into a pile of poop. It has encircled me.

Sometimes in life there are poop piles to be avoided, circumvented, retreated from, but other times, you just have to hold your breath, put one foot in front of the other and tread right through the piles of muck, they cannot be avoided. I am there.

This person I was talking to said her pastor, Pastor Dean (I hope it is okay to copy his word), calls them "Crapertunities". Oh man I love this word! He was able to put into a word what I am feeling.

Crapertunities are the opportunity to go through the mud and mire with an outlook of expectancy, remember our 'expectancy' word from a couple weeks ago? The very messy mess in front of us is an opportunity to bring some good, light, and hope into a dismal, disheartening and stinky situation.

We all have them right? Crapertunities

Whenever you find yourself thinking in your head, or out loud: "Oh shoot"; "Oh crap"; "Oh brother"; "Oh sh**" you have just found yourself in a Crapertunity situation.

For example when I dump my water bottle, coffee, or tea over inside my car and exclaim, "Oh shoot", or rather what a Crapertunity. I can let this ruin my day or decide my car needed cleaning anyways, a reversal of the "poop".

What about the 'big' stuff, my hubby calls and says he is out of a job; my friend calls and says she has been diagnosed with a heart problem; a car accident.... You name it, what if instead of calling them problems, we called them Crapertunities.

The choice is ours to decide how to handle these poop piles. I for one am still learning this lesson! We can get discouraged, give up, whine, complain, get frustrated, and blow a gasket..... Or we can choose to think, what would be helpful in this situation, what is plan B, who needs some encouragement, who could help me, what would make this better and decide to handle the messy situation with a new attitude. I know I tend to hover around the negative instead of on the positive side; that is the crap part of "crapertunity".

God uses poop piles as an opportunity – the "tunity" part of the word, to refine, stretch and add growth to our life to make us more like Himself. What a cool concept that only God could come up with, let's take a poop pile and make it into an opportunity to become better, a character builder or a teachable moment if you will.

James 1: 2-3
"Consider it pure joy, my brothers and sisters, whenever you face trials of many kinds, because you know that the testing of your faith produces perseverance."

I always wondered how you do this because in my mind joy and trials did not go together, a weird kind of pairing; kind of like peanut butter and lettuce, but you know what? One time I tried peanut butter and lettuce in a sandwich and I absolutely love it!

Psalm 30:10-12
"Hear, Lord, and be merciful to me;
Lord, be my help."
You turned my wailing into dancing;
you removed my sackcloth and clothed me with joy,
that my heart may sing your praises and not be silent.
Lord my God, I will praise you forever."

The Bible gives us the remedy for Crapertunities:
"Consider it pure joy...." (James 1:2). None of us like messes, not even little ones, but it is easier when we know that opportunities in pain, suffering, confusion and heartache will not be wasted. God never wastes pain, He always uses it to produce something beautiful then perhaps we can face our Crapertunities with a different attitude.

Crapertunity - such a great word!

Is Truth Dead?

I went to the school office to pick up the mail for the library, two magazines had come in: Time and National Geographic.

Now I would have to say that to me, these are world class magazines, to be on the cover of either makes a statement. So I was shocked to see the messages on each cover: "Is Truth Dead" and "The Next Human".

My first response was to say out loud, to no one in particular, "Truth is surely not dead, Truth is a person and He is alive and well" (and that person is Jesus). Intrigued at their logic I had to read what was up and I got enlightened.....

The Time magazine, April 2017, was the "Is Truth Dead" article, it was an expose on Donald Trump, and statements he had and has made during his campaign and since his election. Well I was able to get past the article but not the front of the magazine.

The front was a take from April 8, 1966 when Time did a piece on – Is God Dead? Both covers put out there to the world, is there a God and is there Truth? On both accounts I want to shout a huge bellowing "YES."

Can we please get another cover on Time magazine giving an emphatic "YES" with stories to go with it.... It is only fair to give the alternate view if they want to ask the question – just saying?

The National Geographic April 2017 magazine, the cover picture depicts a primitive ape man going forward to a robotic man. The one article, "Beyond Human by D. T.

Max": *"Like any other species, we are the product of millions of years of evolution. Now we're taking matters into our own hands."* What a scary thought, mankind has not done well in history and now we are taking matters into our own hands?

The question they ask is *"Is man still evolving?"* Their answer: *"Yes, under the influence of culture and technology."*

"Present Day and Near Future Do-It-Yourself Evolution" – for me this still does not prove evolution rather that man is trying to prove evolution by his own fix it methods.....

The article states: *"Now we're developing powerful new gene-editing tools that could bring about human-directed evolution. Most research has been on other organisms – for instance, attempting to change a mosquito genome so the insect cannot transmit Zika or malaria. We could harness the same techniques to "design" our babies – simply choose a preferred hair or eye color. But should we? "There's definitely a dark side," says bioethicist Linda MacDonald Glenn, "but I do think humanity-plus is inevitable. We are, by our nature, tinkerers."*

The whole article/section was long so I have just highlighted some parts but the following are items mentioned in the article: natural selection, human enhancements, embryo selection and choosing the most intelligent embryo, or the ability to choose which desirable traits – eye color, hair color, even being able to duplicate desirable embryos. The article does mention the scary fact of "who sets the bar?" (to decide what is desirable, will the country with the most money win?)

"More than 50 years ago two scientists coined the word "cyborg" for an imaginary organism – part human, part machine. It seemed science fiction, but today people have implants embedded into their skin that can unlock doors or log into their computers without touching anything. Neil Harbisson, who can perceive colors only by transforming them into sounds he can hear through an antenna implanted in his head.

From prosthetics to pharmaceuticals, humans have been using technology to alter their physical and mental capabilities for thousands of years. Now, with our rapid advances in technology, some people are embracing human augmentation as a means of expressing themselves and experiencing the world in a totally different way."

One company – "Dangerous Things has sold over 10,000 RFID (Radio–frequency identification devices) chips as well as do-it-yourself kits. The people who buy them call themselves body hackers or grinders."

I looked up Dangerous Things and was astonished at their product line: *"Custom gadgetry for the discerning biohacker". "We believe that biohacking is the next phase in human evolution."*

They sell RFID's - 4 kinds to be exact. What can you do with them?

"*Our x-series transponders are the most popular transponder implants because they are easily installed using an injection assembly (a needle). Because they are installed using a needle, we partner with professional body piercers to ensure our customers can get our products installed safely by a licensed professional in a sterile studio environment. Our flex transponders are more advanced, with better performance, but installation requires a medical doctor or a skilled and licensed professional body modification artist who is familiar with more advanced body modification procedures.*

For humans, it typically means replacing keys and passwords... identity as applied to access control. Dangerous Things team members use their transponders to enter their homes, unlock and start their vehicles, log into computers, etc. The specifics of how you can accomplish those actions depends on the thing you want to access, ability to hack/update it, and the transponder you have." *https://dangerousthings.com*

 For as low as $39.00 I can order an injectable RFID Kit, complete with the needle to place it under my skin or pay $200 for the Flex transponders and have a body piercer or Dr. place it there. Reading these 2 articles was almost traumatizing, **we have arrived my friends.** We have kicked God off the throne and decided it was time man took over from baby making to human making and we have assisted suicide to choose when we end life. These have always been God decisions, but I guess we think we know better.

I know my Bible well enough to know that God will only allow us to go so far before He decides it has to stop, so

the questions rolling around in my mind ..... what will
He do and when and heaven help us if He does not.

Our Good Samaritans

Did you ever have that "feeling" that forewarns you that something is about to happen? That sense that you have to go forward but you know there will be a toll. I had it but I had to go anyways, it is something good or bad....or both?

I have not been able to cry for a few months, I want too, many times, but it just will not spill out or come up and over or however you want to name it. I know for me that when that happens, I am usually on "survival" mode. I have been too busy, too involved, too stressed or too something and my body shifts into a mode that enables me to keep on going, but not feel a whole heck of a lot. It is not a healthy place for me to stay in, but it is "safe" for a short while.

Our journey this past weekend meant driving 23 hours or 2300 kilometers from Friday morning to Sunday night, loading up a household, moving my son and his wife from city to city, then unloading it at this end. Health issues have prevented him from being able to lift anything, they needed help; and so we went. We were bringing some muscle and the trailer to load up their belongings for the move.

When we first went to pick up the 16' trailer we were quickly halted when only a 12' trailer was left. There was no way it would hold their belongings. We went home deflated and wondering what to do since there was no rental places open. My husband called his boss and he graciously let us use his personal trailer, a 18' one. Our first miracle.

We got to Hinton and realized our truck was acting up, when we would idle down the truck would shake, and sputter, and this, just the first leg of the journey. My husband bought a code reader and we plugged it into the motor – 5 warning codes popped up. Turns out it was the Cam Shifter Positioning Sensor. We bought one and installed it in the parking lot, the codes went away and the truck ran perfectly.

We continued on…. by the time we hit Kamloops the truck was definitely not a happy unit. The engine was missing and still sputtering and shaking. We pulled into Canadian Tire and plugged the code reader back in. The same codes, but only 2 of them popped up again. The service department had closed 15 minutes prior to our arrival.

We called a few people for ideas and the consensus was to test the alternator. We did and it proved to be not functioning properly. We bought a new alternator (not a cheap item) and attempted to install it in the Canadian Tire parking lot. 3 Hours we were there, the dogs and I took turns sitting on the ground in the parking lot, or me, helping Brian work on the truck or doing a parts run inside the store.

Only one person stopped by to talk to us in the first 2 ½ hours. She was from the motor home parked behind us. They live in Penticton and had literally just bought the motor home that morning. It had started fine at the people's house but after they drove it away, the thing would not start again. They had to sit in the parking lot all night until the service department opened back up. She was due at a dog show in Kelowna so she was heading out in a rental car, but her husband would stay with the motor home. We wished each other the best and I assured her that if we had to stay the night, we would head over to her hubby for visiting.

We managed to lose a screw for the guard over the alternator so I ran back inside the store to try to find one in the parts department. The man there reading his magazine barely looked up at me and just said, "Nope, hardware". I had to ask him where that was, aisle 27, and then he resumed reading. I, at this point was covered with dust and dirt, I had climbed into the motor, under the motor looking for the screw. At some point I prayed that God would send us someone to help us.

I found the aisle and attempted to find what I needed, I finally found a young fellow, who I thought probably would be no help, but he turned out to be the best helper ever. He went out of his way to help me but in the end it was a machine screw and they did not sell those, except in the parts department. I told him that the other guy said "nope". This guy said they used to so on our way by we would look where they used to be. They did not sell them, but he found something we could bandaid it together with until we could find the right one.

The new alternator was almost in place when I got back, my husband was trying to get it in, bolt it down and get the belt back on. A native man strolled over complete with cowboy hat and asked us if we needed help. Brian was having a horrible time getting a couple bolts in – this fellow said we needed an extension bar to make the job easier. Brian was attempting to move a wire out of the way and touched the new alternator with a metal bar. The arc of electricity that shot out of the new alternator was huge. All 3 of us stood there silent for a minute or so, then the new fellow said, "I think you just wrecked your new alternator. When they get shorted like that they are usually done." He went on to say he had never seen one work after an arc like that. He felt we should reattach everything and then test the alternator to see if indeed it was wrecked or not. I know both Brian and I felt like crying at this point. Our new friend said that he needed a new extension bar anyways so he would go buy one and let us use it.

After our fellow went into the store, I came up beside Brian and said "Let's lay hands on this alternator and ask God to make it work". We prayed for a miracle. I said to my husband at this point, "We need a Steve," Brian nodded. Brian has 2 amazing friends named Steve and they are both amazing and logical at working out problems and figuring out how to make things work and had helped us out in so many situations, we were feeling the void at that moment.

The fellow came back with the extension bar and in seconds we got the bolts and belt back on, it made the job so much easier.

We went to give him the bar back and he said "I don't need it, you do. I already have one at home."

I replied, "But you said you needed one."

He told us, "I only told you that, I knew you needed it, so I bought it for you."

We offered to pay him for the $50 item and he flatly refused. We started the truck and then tested the alternator, it worked! Our new friend stared at the motor and said he could not believe the alternator was working, it did not make sense. Brian said – "It is a miracle."

I came over to our new friend and said, "What is your name?"

He stuck out his hand and said, "My name is Steve."

At that point I started to cry.

I wish I could say the trip was amazing after that but it was not; from having too much stuff to load into the trailer; to having to rent a 2nd trailer; to having the hottest day to load up the Okanagan has seen this year; to running out of gas 10 minutes out of Valemont; and having the truck acting up at times still.

But when I would get discouraged I would think of our new friend "Steve"; the young fellow at Canadian Tire; or friends in a city we were passing through waiting there with truck parts as we went by and smile. I believe they were all a direct answer to my prayers: Send someone to help (we got several); We needed a Steve.

God was listening. He does not always make life clear sailing, in fact, often life is really hard and tough, but He was letting me know He was there and He was with us.

The running out of gas story: God encouraged a lady at 8:00 am Sunday morning that she needed smokes and she found us broken down at the bottom of her hill. She whipped her car around and came back inside 5 minutes with a full jerry can of gas that she just happened to have on hand back at her house.

God can and does use anyone, you just never know when you will need the "good Samaritan" or be the "good Samaritan" for someone else, you just might be the person God uses to encourage others on their journey. We are so very grateful for all of ours!

Lifter of Our Heads

I heard 2 other sermons this past week alluding to this same subject: whenever that happens I know that God is trying to get our attention about something.

The subject was keeping our heads down.

Now under some circumstances keeping your head down can be helpful, even lifesaving, but in this case, keeping your head down means you are downward focused, usually focused on ourselves and our own problems.

My chiropractor told me that we are in an unprecedented time of treating more and more people for neck and back injuries. He said the amount of surgeries on young people has raised considerably, the reason, he told me, was: computers and cell phones.

He said even glasses not positioned correctly on your face requiring you have to move or tilt your head to see clearly can cause huge issues with your neck, now that we can order glasses on line this could have potential problems.

At first I wondered at the validity of his words but then I thought about it – probably while I was texting on my phone. When we are on our phones are heads are bent down. I started looking around, sure enough people's heads all around me were down when they are texting, or looking at items on their phones. Take a look around you at people on their phones – their necks are bent forward and very few of the people you look at are actively engaged in conversation with each other. The looking down isolates us, it helps us to focus strictly on "me", in my own little world.

I guess the analogy is fairly straight forward on this one: if you are on your phone, you are oblivious to the world around you and your focus is pointed down. Oh because you are "on your phone", you might think you are "connected" but the people and things sitting around you are being ignored.

As I drove through Jasper this weekend I marveled at the Rocky Mountains once again. They are so beautiful. I wondered what it is about mountains that compels and fascinates us so much; people come from all over the world to view them.   Is it the jagged rocks and crags; the snowcapped tops, the mosaic of foliage covering the mountainside? Honestly it is probably all of it. But whatever it is, it raises our heads and we stare in awe at the majestic wonder that is our mountains.

I do not think it coincidence that mountains tend to make us raise our heads and eyes. God wants us to lift our eyes up, towards Him, it makes sense that our eyes long to look up, albeit mountains, clouds, stars, the sky and to catch a glimpse of God, the one who created it all.

Psalm 3:3
"But You, O LORD, are a shield about me, My glory, and the One who lifts my head."

As you trod along in life with your eyes cast down, you might find a little change on the sidewalk but in the long run, but you will not be living in the sense of awe and wonder that raising your focus upwards can give you.

"Look unto me, and be saved, all the ends of the earth: for I Am God, and there is none else." Psalm 45:22
God wants our focus "up!"..... "Look unto me..."

In the Bible when the Israelite's left Egypt they were on their way to Israel, the Promised Land, however they ended up in the desert for 40 years. The trip should have only taken 11 days, but their attitude and behavior got them 40 years.

At first they rejoiced that they were free but then the desert began to feel like a prison as well. They looked around them *(not up)* grumbled and complained, there is no food or water; they looked around them but *not up,* they complained to God, why did you bring us here to die? They were mad at God and started to let Him have it!

God sent snakes into the camp and people got bit and some of them died, well that changed their tune rather quickly. They humbled themselves and apologized to God and asked Him to come heal them. He did, but the way He did it is a little odd.

He told them to make a snake from bronze and put it up on a pole, anyone who got bit could go, look up at it, and live. How bizarre! But they did it and it worked.

We are no different than the Israelite's. I mean, honestly, if it had been us instead of them, we would have taken the same detoured 40 year path, whining and complaining. We, as human beings, tend to forget our blessings almost as fast as they come. We tend to focus on the negatives, not the positives. We keep our heads down, nose to the grind stone, and focus on the things that are not really going to help us in the long run.

Why do we need God when we can look down at our phone and either Google it, ask Siri or check on Wikipedia and get the answers by ourselves?

Why is it so important to raise our eyes? Why does God want us to raise our heads?

Jesus said, in John 3:14: "Just as Moses lifted up the snake in the desert, so the Son of Man must be lifted up."

Today we must do exactly what the Israelites had to do centuries ago. Look up at Jesus, nailed to the cross and acknowledge He can save us and that He has the answers we need. In humbling ourselves, we must admit that there is nothing we can do to save ourselves. No amount of human effort can ever save us or have all the answers.

My thought is this: we can continue to have our heads bowed low and study our phones, or whatever it is that keeps our focus down, including our grumbling about our problems OR we can raise our heads, lift our eyes and keep our focus upwards towards to the Creator who created everything and has answers to our every problem.

One way frees us and one way weighs us down (and hurts your neck), you get to decide which is best for you.

Good Grief

There is a word out there that not many people know what to do with – Grief.

Actually people know the word, they do not know how to do the process of grief. We hear it bounced back and forth as something we should and need to do, but what exactly is "grief"?

There was a time I got an excruciating pain in the top of my one leg that filtered right into my abdomen and down my leg in a way that sent me to the hospital. The pain was fierce, a shock wave of terror letting loose inside my body that was out of control.

After spending the day on morphine and running a battery of tests, they could not find anything physically wrong with me. After a day or so the pain went away, but I was left with the thought of what on earth had caused that pain and feared it would come back.

I was scheduled to see a counsellor that week for another reason and briefly mentioned the hospital visit in passing and she told me that the word that came to her was "grief". Now I was totally ready to throw that definition out the window because how could the two be related?!

We prayed but the word stayed with me and it was like God would not let it leave. I took some time and pondered about "grief". I did have some things that I had to deal with and then I came across this little book I had stuffed in a drawer: *"Experiencing Grief"* by H. Norman Wright ©2004 H. Norman Wright Published by B & H Publishing Group.

I picked it up and started to read, it is a small little book, 85 pages in length; I found it informative and wished everyone could read it, but it was not really for me, you know what I mean?

Then I turned to page 45.....

"I told God I was angry,
I thought He'd be surprised.
I thought I'd kept hostility
quite cleverly disguised.

I told the Lord I hate Him.
I told Him that I hurt.
I told Him that He isn't fair,
He's treated me like dirt.

I told God I was angry
But I'm the one surprised.
"What I've known all along," He said,
"you've finally realized."

"At last you have admitted
what's really in your heart.
Dishonesty, not anger
was keeping us apart.

"Even when you hate Me,
I don't stop loving you.
Before you can receive that love
you must confess what's true.

"In telling me the anger
you genuinely feel.
It loses power over you,
permitting you to heal."

I told God I was sorry
And He's forgiven me.
The truth that I was angry
has finally set me free."

Jessica Shaver
(Footnote in Experiencing Grief: Excerpt taken from
Under His Wings by Patsy Clairmont,
www.healinghouse.org)

I can tell you the tears that had been pent up for some
time broke loose when I read this poem and a dam burst
inside me. Someone had read my deepest most intimate
thoughts and what was even more miraculous, God
knew too!

With any loss in our life, job, marriage, children, health,
money, pets...... if we are truly honest, we want a chat
with God because we need to ask Him, 'Where were you
that day?' Or 'Hey God, did you see what just
happened?' Losses rock our world and cause us to
question God's goodness and shake our faith in Him to
our very core. It causes us to question Gods'
trustworthiness. We find we cannot sing those "God is
good" songs because we are not really sure at the
moment.

But grief is good, it is the only way you will move on.

The opening illustration of this blog above gives us the
stages of grief, counsellors and websites all talk about
the "stages" of grief. Nice neat stages.

Then there was the picture that I identified with.....the
messy one.

I was the mess and because it was a visual aid that said it was okay to be a "mess". I got it... I was OKAY even if I was messy. There is no proper way to grieve. Yes there are stages, patterns you will go through but they are NOT in order and you might go through All or Some and some over and over and lots at the same time. Grief can be messy and probably will be, life is messy too.

What I learned was NOT grieving and keeping that pain inside can cause physical damage and pain to other parts of our body. When we are experience loss of any kind, we have to get it out in a healthy way because if we do not, it will come out itself in a physical way.

Let me give you a couple tidbits from the "Experiencing Grief" book:

- "In a culture that does not like to acknowledge loss or talk about the impact, it's difficult to grieve. And when we add this silence to the fact that most of us have never been taught the process and normalcy of grief, no wonder we struggle."   Page 1
- "In grief, the bottom falls out of your world." Page 3
- "With any loss comes grief, and a companion of grief is pain. The pain of grief can be overwhelming. It's like a visitor who has overstayed his welcome." Page 9
- "Grieving is a disorderly process. You won't control it, nor can you schedule its expression." Page 11
- "Along this difficult journey many experience what we call a "grief spasm." It's alarming since it's an intense upsurge of grief that happens suddenly and when least expected." Page 18
- "Guilt and shame walk their way into the grief process.... There is a sense of sadness, depression and despair." Page 40 and 48

- "It's like learning to swim. You have to step into the water to begin the process." Page 68

Oh my friends, grief is messy and it hurts. Truly if you have something to grieve or if you have had losses in your life, it hurts already, even if you do not acknowledge it. If this subject has touched or affected you in any way, I would ask that you consider talking to a counsellor, a trusted friend and getting a copy of the little "Experiencing Grief" booklet.

The really awesome thing about grief is that we each, yes, every one of us, will experience grief at some point or points in our life, we are surrounded by others who have been through it. While grief is an individual process and we each travel it differently, it is good consolation to know others have traveled it and survived.

The Unseen

Look at this picture, it is a landscape with the snowcapped mountains, the forest, the water in the foreground, trees, bush, grass; we took this picture on the way up to Liard Hot Springs. It is a beautiful shot, whenever I drive through the mountains I think to myself, God created such beauty and majesty, I do not know how people can not acknowledge God with the beauty all around them.

But it struck me suddenly as I looked at this picture what is not there.

What do I mean by that? We look at the overall picture the beautiful landscape. Up on those mountains, there are probably deer, moose, there might even be mountain goats, or mountain sheep. Possibly as well, squirrels, birds, chipmunks, cougars, bears, and in the water we cannot see the fish, the beavers, the otters, or the muskrats. Just because they do not show up in the photograph and we cannot see them, does it mean they are not there? Of course not.

It is kind of like that saying, if a tree falls in the forest and no one is there to hear it, does it make a sound? Of course it makes a sound, any tree coming down, makes a sound.

Just because you cannot see the animals, it does not mean they are not there. God pressed upon me that He is in charge of every animal in that forest. He knows what they are going through, He knows what they need to survive, He knows the food they need to eat, He knows where to have their babies, when to have their babies and where to get shelter from the storms. He has got that all under control, and just because I cannot see it does not mean He is not working there just like it does not mean the animals are not there either.

In my life, when I cannot see the hand of God, when I cannot feel the hand of God, do I believe God is working? Or like this picture do I take it on face value and say nice picture, it is just a bunch of trees and water, without knowing the true depth of what the human eye cannot see.

What about when life "hits"? Last week we talked about grief, the emotional toils of life losses which inevitably will happen and I wonder where God is.

For me, in my life, sometimes I have to look at the bigger picture. I have to get outside my box, get outside what my eyes can see and focus on what God has said. He has said He would take care of the animals of the field (Job 38). He said if a swallow falls to the ground He knows it (Matthew 10:29). He knows the hairs on our head (Luke 12:7). He said He would take care of me.

Will I continue to believe and walk in faith when I cannot see His unseen presence with my human eyes?

Hmmmm good question!

A Family In Grief

We are grief-stricken in my family this week.

What should have been a joyous occasion suddenly turned somber, horrendous and painful beyond our thinking.

I am going to be a grandma and we have been so excited, celebrating the expectation of a new little family member. According to pregnancy protocol the 1st ultrasound is at 3 months and then you see the baby doctor. Last week was that marker and we all anticipated being sent a text picture of the ultrasound picture announcing this new little life.

They could not find a heartbeat. The new little life that had started out blooming, was not going to grow anymore.

Much to my amazement and that of others was the procedure that followed. This young couple, going to the appointment with joy and expectation, was then told the announcement of no heartbeat and to proceed directly to emergency. No other explanations, so no time to grieve this news or even try to comprehend what was happening – they sat for 4 hours in emerge waiting to see a doctor. No privacy to cry, to try to understand what was happening, surrounded on all sides by others who were hurting with their own injuries, but no safe place to absorb this news.

The emergency doctor was very gracious and kind, he wanted them to see a baby doctor and that would be another 2 and ½ hours before that happened. They waited, not sure of what else to do, the total of 6 and ½ hours, numbed off to the pain of the obvious.

The baby doctor was awesome, answering and reassuring this couples questions and providing facts.

This type of miscarriage is very common, according to statistics, it happens in 1 out of 6 pregnancies. But this doctor, cautioned us that doctors believe it happens more often than that because it often happens at home with no doctor involved and that it could be as high as 1 in 3 pregnancies. There is nothing anyone could have done differently to prevent it, it happens.

We all have been grieving in our own way; we are not ready to talk about it just yet so thank you for understanding this.

God reminded me that He formed me, you, all of us, in our mother's womb, a person right from the time of conception. (Psalm 119)

This baby is not forgotten, God knows. I can sit and blame God for the "why's" or I can place my trust in Him that this little person will be in heaven when I get there – because nothing and *no one* escapes His attention. *I am a grandma and I will meet my grand baby when I get there of this I have no doubt.*

Psalm 139: 13 "For you created my inmost being; you knit me together in my mother's womb."

Jeremiah 1:5 "Before I formed you in the womb I knew you, before you were born I set you apart..."

Final Farewell From the Library

The thoughts in this blog are for everyone, the ending is specifically for "the gang" – you know who you are. The 1st part I saw on Facebook and I felt I needed a place to share it, and I had an opening.....

I think they should be teaching this in school:

Life Rules

Life is not divided into semesters – you will not get the summers off

School may have done away with winners and losers, life has not

Television and cell phones are not real life, people actually have to leave those to go to real jobs and talk to real people

If you are born poor it is not your mistake, if you die poor it is your mistake

Life is not fair

You will not make $60,000 a year right out of high school

If you think your teacher was tough, wait until you get a boss

Flipping burgers is not beneath your dignity

Be nice to nerds, chances are you will end up working for one

The world will not care about your self-esteem

*My addition: you will have to learn to balance your own money, there is no money tree

MRS WHEELERS LIBRARY RULES:

Remember the Library Rules, they will work well for you in your job and family situations:

Remember to use only Library language, no swears ("Oh my stars" is acceptable in most places)

Remember to be kind

Remember that gossip will not be tolerated

Remember to be truthful, but only with love, no snarkiness

Remember you can still love someone and not like their behaviour

Remember that you matter

Remember to befriend the lonely

Remember to work hard

Remember to respect yourself

Remember that you are needed

Remember that the world does not owe you, you owe the world, strive to make it a better place

Remember that you were a gift to this librarian

As you are released into the world to find and make your own way, remember that you do not have to always follow the mold, as a matter of fact – break it, because you are each unique with your own gifts and talents and uniqueness stands out.

Know that the world can be a magical place, but it can also seem harsh and insensitive. There will be days where you will soar and think it could not get any better and there will be days where you wonder if you can do it. How can you possibly keep going...

It is at those moments if you take a minute, breathe in and out, look up and focus, stay still, in the silence you just might hear a librarian's voice whispering softly: "You got this, you can do it, I know you can. I believe in you."

Also know that somewhere that day a librarian said a prayer for you asking for divine intervention and asking that you someday know how much you are loved by your Creator.

So now, Go – you are released to the world, whether you think you are ready or not...

"Go, You Got This....."

Just A Little Crooked

I have a tree thing. I love trees, the feeling you get when you stand and look up, way up at a tall magnificent tree, or when you stand at the base of a tree, probably a cedar, with a girth so wide you cannot see around it. How about sitting under one on a hot sunny day, relieved as its branches spread over you and offer you cool relief and if you are lucky you can hear the wind flit against the leaves and hear it whisper.

Trees are one of those things in nature that you can take for granted even though they are around us everywhere in some form or another; trees in the mountains, trees in parks, trees in parking lots of the grocery stores.

I came to realize quickly after moving out of British Columbia that I took my trees for granted. In Alberta we do not have the same size of trees here where I live, we have trees but you have to look harder for the really "big" ones. What we do have became very interesting to me and as I studied the trees.

In one park I used to walk in I noticed a large number of trees growing at an angle, not straight up as we think most trees do. They were not twisted or crooked, they were straight but definitely growing directionally challenged. These trees were the ones that made me really take notice and look at the plight of trees. How did they get crooked?

In this picture almost all the trees are growing at an angle, it was not a windy day, nor did I tilt my camera, this is how they grow.

These directionally challenged trees were growing on this angle because of the wind. These trees stood right in the path of an almost constant and steady dose of wind. Sometimes more of a breeze, other times a definite steady wind, often with gusts and then for some days, a squall of sorts, complete with a "northeaster" that would make having a good hair day almost impossible. There was not often a day were these trees did not get some kind of wind pushing against them. It caused the trees to grow on an angle. They might look strange but they still were growing.

I love this tree, I made my husband stop the truck so I could get a picture. This tree and perhaps 2 others grew with a definite curve, the other trees around it were straight.

Either way, straight or crooked, the trees still grow, they still produce their foliage, they still are firmly rooted in the ground, the crooked ones probably even more so than other trees, because they have had to hang on for their very existence, they just look a little different.

Is that not just like people, these trees remind me of people.

I mean all of us have had some "push back" or pressure when life hit us now and again, for the most part we can bend and sway and take it, regain ourselves and keep on growing. No one looking at us would know we had been hit.

Then for others, life comes in waves, it "pushes back" on a regular basis, this might cause us to sway and bend for longer periods of time. And for some, life seems to be a continuous "push back", we regularly face the pressure of blustery winds, we have a hard time growing against the pressure, but we do it.

When life pushes against you, you start to lean for the pressure is great. The leaning might be temporary, as in a tree swaying with the wind. The leaning might be more pronounced like a tree bowing down to the ground or the leaning might be so constant that the tree grows at an angle. For some, just like a tree that cannot withstand the fiercest winds, they snap off and fall to the ground. The pressure of life and wind is just too hard.

Can you tell by looking at a forest which trees will withstand the next gale? Not usually, although sometimes looking at their fruit or foliage will give us signs of weakening.

When we survey people, we cannot see if they have been hit by a breeze, a wind or even a gust. Others we can tell, have deep roots, life has hit them hard and they are solidly grounded, they might not stand quite so tall and straight, but those are the ones who usually have branches they can spread over others to help and protect them on their way to recovery.

Consider what are we rooted in and how deep do our roots go? Are we ready to stand and face the next gusty gale that is headed our way?

God says He wants to be our deep root – nothing that happens to us is out of His watchful eye. We might not like it, we might even hate it, but like the trees that grow under pressure, the deeper our roots grow, the more solid we stand, even if we look a little crooked.

A Hot Topic

This is not the blog I had originally planned to put here but when I was praying about what to write and waiting for a subject, this one became the "hot topic" that was impressed on me to talk about.

As I regarded this map of the current (Tuesday July 11) fires in the province of BC I was astounded. I think living here in Alberta and probably anywhere outside of BC, we get the "short version" of the BC fires, I mean we know it is bad, but when I opened the map at the following link and opened the *interactive map* – I was stunned:

http://www2.gov.bc.ca/gov/content/safety/wildfire-status

Basically the whole province is on fire (except the island): the red dots mean brand new fires (you cannot see most of these on the above map as they are mainly in the east corner blocked from the picture) started within 24 hours; the flaming yellow red fires are "fires of note"; and the little orange/yellow dots are active fires.

I sat there staring and then had to go onto Alberta's wildfire status map: Yellow are fires being held and green are fires under control. NO red ones.

Quite the difference.

This week we are planning a family wedding, and we have family coming from BC, our family itself is from BC and my heart goes out to ALL of BC and the residents who are watching their surroundings burn down around them.

I was not surprised that the first people to rally to the BC residents plight as Fort Mac people. They get it they understand and they are pouring out the aid to help their neighbors.

Here is another vital link to use to find out how you can help or volunteer or to pass onto folks who may be in need of help: it tells you how to register with Red Cross, how to get help for medical/prescriptions because you had to leave fast and could not grab them, to help for the evacuees, help to shelter animals and livestock, food donation and food banks, shelters and evacuation sites, finding other people and making financial donations.

http://globalnews.ca/news/3584929/b-c-wildfires-2017-how-you-can-help/

One easy thing anyone can do is text the word: word: fires to 45678 and $10 will be donated to the BC Fire Fund with the Red Cross, any carrier will do it and it is easy and we can all do that. I tried it, it works and totally something we can all do.

I am not sure what action I will take to try to help my home province and friends, but I encourage you to prayerfully consider what action you will take and not just sit back and watch the fire scenes explode across your television but actually put some action to this request and if you already done so – God Bless You!

So A Gay Guy Walks Into a Christian Bookstore

I was asked to write a blog on the Judgement of God. When I was first asked, I thought "heck no, that sounds like brimstone and fire!" but when they explained what they were thinking, I thought... hmmmmm...

The person explained that people and God both judge people. But people judgement and God judgement are totally different.

People Judging	God Judging
Critical	True but not condemning
Pulls away & rejects others	God draws & gets close
Shaming	God never shames
Hurts	Hurts, but in a good way
People tend to never forget	God says He will not remember
People point fingers	God points to the cross
No offer of help, just heartache	Offers solutions & restoration
No Love offered until you shape up	God offers Love just the way you are

The thing of it is, when people judge other people, they are actually deciding to judge God as well.

People and God judge differently, so in choosing a different way, people are saying that God is wrong and they are right. This basically puts God on trial for His version of judgement.

Let me explain with a true story:

Guy walks into a Christian Bookstore somewhere in Canada. He says to the older, mature lady working behind the counter, "Where would your section be on how to help separate yourself from your children?"

She says, "If I might ask, what exactly are you looking for?"

He says, "Well it's been a long three months, 2 of my children have tried to kill themselves in the past three months."

She exclaims, "Oh my! Are you attending a church that can help you?"

He says, "Well, no. I tried that and it did not work out well."

Interested she queries, "What happened?"

"I told them I was gay and they basically turned their backs on me."

Incredulous she says, "If I might be so bold to suggest that perhaps your children are reacting to your choices in life."

He says, "Look, I have spent over $100,000 in counselors, Christian and otherwise, trying to figure out what's wrong with me. No one could figure it out. I know God knows, but I sure as hell know you do not. But what I have discovered is that well-meaning Christians, like yourself, tell me what is wrong with me and they think they know how to fix me. I have been prayed over, anointed, prayed about, ridiculed, insulted, shunned and told what a sinner I am.

All I know is that God can figure me out and when I try to go to church, so called Christians just point their fingers, gossip and condemn me for my sin. *We never get to talk about theirs.* So I think I will skip church and just keep talking to God, cause He knows just what to do with me. Now can you show me that section or not?"

And that my friends, is how God and people differ.

You see God gave us one rule: "Love the Lord your God with all your heart, soul and mind and love your neighbor as yourself."

But often we will not love our neighbor because they are different: perhaps a different skin color, a different religion, a different set of family values, a different language, a different money class or they do not handle life the way we do.

God did not say "Love your neighbors who are like you". He said "Love your neighbors as yourself".

If you need help knowing who your neighbor is try reading the Good Samaritan story in the Bible; it is pretty clear. Luke 10:25-37

How do you love? Do you relate to the guy in the story, condemned for your life choices or with the lady behind the counter who judges her neighbor by her standards (or rules)?

Both of these people are "sinners", actually I have yet to meet a person who isn't: yet we love to point our fingers and judge other people's sin.

I love the way Dylan Bressey explained it to me, he is the local director of Young Life, a booming teen group here in Grande Prairie. He said the kids will come to him and say, "I'm bi-sexual" or "I don't believe in God." He says, "That's okay, you are welcome here. Hey can I talk to you about this guy Jesus?" and he talks about Jesus and loves on them and he lets God sort out all that other stuff. **Brilliant!**

I, for years, was probably more like the lady behind the counter if I was honest.

Years ago God got hold of me and told me, while I was at my most miserable, most sinful, most not walking the right road. Then, at my ugliest, was when He loved me the most. It was incredulous and life changing. It changed my view, my perspective about how look at others and how God looks at us.

You see, God does not love us because we are good. God loves us because He is good.
A vast difference.

He does not ever ask you to shape up before He will love you!

Can I ask you a personal question that you can answer to yourself? You do not need to tell anyone.

I wanted to ask, do you judge? But that question is almost redundant, even though in the Bible it says explicitly not to judge, we all judge other people to some degree.

Rather I will ask, how do you judge?
Like God, with only Love?
OR, like people – with only criticism?

A Deceptively Sweet Mystery

A good mystery has to have drama, intrigue, a lot of unanswered questions and of course a villain. The following quote (albeit I left out a couple of words to create a great case of a who-dun-it) has it all:

"The question has baffled scientists for nearly a decade. Around the world . . . tens of thousands are suddenly empty. They have vanished, abandoning their homes and ominously never returning. No corpses found on the scene. No clues left behind.

"One day, they are in; the next, they're gone," said Hartmut Doebel, assistant professor, "and nobody has a good explanation for how it happened."

Now the "who" ....

Dubbed colony collapse disorder (CCD), the mysterious malady has claimed 40 percent of the world's honeybees since it was first identified in 2006. Almost half of the bees in the United States have disappeared in just a decade." *The Continuing Plight of the Honeybee,* June 2, 2015 by John Diconsiglio

Yup, it Bees, more than that it is the Honeybee, domestic and wild. If you watch the news, read a newspaper, browse through Time or National Geographic, you have no doubt heard of the plight of the honeybee. If you have not heard about it, let me give you the buzz on it...

Why should this concern you? About 1/3 of our worldwide food production is at risk because we are losing our honeybees at an alarming rate.

In 2015 it was estimated that beekeepers worldwide lost about 45% of their bees and in 2016 it was estimated to be around 60%.

What does this mean for you and me? It means less food and I am not just talking about honey. Bees are also producers of bee pollen, royal jelly, and bee propolis and each of these four items have amazing and healing qualities to them (but that is another blog).

In addition to producing cool stuff, bees pollinate about 1/3 of our food worldwide, from fruit to nuts to coffee beans.

I first heard about the strange and random dying off of honeybees back in the early 2000's when I attended a conference with the health food store I was managing. The speaker was from Switzerland where they were already doing intense research on the disappearing honeybees. North American was not yet on board with the honeybee prognosis but in Europe the alarm was raised and in fact the EU has taken measures to ban the use of pesticides.

I had also watched a documentary where in China they have to hand pollinate their fruit trees, they had to keep their children home from school in blossom season. Check this out:

"The most dramatic example comes from the apple and pear orchards of south west China, where wild bees have been eradicated by excessive pesticide use and a lack of natural habitat. In recent years, farmers have been forced to hand-pollinate their trees, carrying pots of pollen and paintbrushes with which to individually pollinate every flower, and using their children to climb up to the highest blossoms. This is clearly just possible for this high-value crop, but there are not enough humans in the world to pollinate all of our crops by hand." *Decline of Honeybees Forces China's Apple Farmers to Pollinate By Hand*, Dave Goulson, 02.10.2012

The mystery continues, scientists are not 100% sure why the bees are dying off, probably it is a combination of factors. There are several thoughts on why this is die off is occurring. It is thought that chemicals, most likely pesticides could cause the demise of our honeybees.

Other presented theories are: loss of habitat, climate change, which changes the plants and flowers, and disease. Pathogens carried by mites weaken bees, which makes them susceptible to pesticide poisoning.

Solutions:
"There are simple solutions; studies in Europe and North America have found that planting strips of wildflowers on farms, and leaving patches of natural vegetation such as forests, can greatly boost pollinator populations. These practices can also increase populations of natural predators, decreasing the need for pesticide sprays." *Decline of Honeybees Forces China's Apple Farmers To Pollinate By Hand*, Dave Goulson, 02.10.2012

"The thing we can most control is pesticides," says Sass. Anyone with outdoor space, from a container garden to a large lawn, can create a pesticide-free, safe space for pollinators that will encourage native bees and other beneficial insects.

We can also make sure to purchase plants that are not pretreated with pesticides by asking questions when we shop for seeds and flowers. We can let our lawns grow a bit longer and leave the blooming clover for bees to enjoy. We can ask our elected officials to pass county and town ordinances to reduce pesticide spraying, and we can urge corporations to stop making and selling neonicotinoids." *The Buzz About Colony Collapse Disorder*, December 31, 2015 Alexandra Zissu

"We can at least do our part by plating bee-friendly plants, including Echinacea, lavender, and clover, while also becoming aware of the impact that our food choices could have on the health of not only honey bees, but the food system that supports us." *National Post,* Jennifer Sygo, August 1, 2014

Beekeeping is now "trendy" and in some areas of North America, backyard bee hives are popping up, from starting or building your own to renting a hive (check out the Heritage Bee Company), or having bee hives in the gardens atop of towering skyscrapers or hotels.

Some San Francisco hotels have built beehives on their rooftops – NBC News
link: http://www.nbcnews.com/slideshow/san-francisco-hotels-build-buzz-eco-efforts-rooftop-beehives-n575081

What do London's Buckingham Palace, New York's Whitney Museum of American Art and the Notre-Dame Cathedral in Paris all have in common?

They're all keepers of honeybees, part of a growing collection of bee-friendly landmarks around the world. CNN Link: http://www.cnn.com/travel/article/honey-bee-hotels/index.html

If you want to find out what plants are great for pollination in your growing area, check out The Xerces Society for each growing area in the USA and they have a link for Canada.

Xerces Link: http://www.xerces.org/pollinator-conservation/plant-lists/

The David Suzuki Foundation also has some ideas: Link: http://www.davidsuzuki.org/what-you-can-do/food-and-our-planet/create-a-bee-friendly-garden/

If we all do something to help the plight of the bees, we help ourselves, our food, our neighbors and the busy little bees – and truly, that is a really sweet spot to be in.

Links to Read more:

http://news.nationalgeographic.com/news/2013/13/130510-honeybee-bee-science-european-union-pesticides-colony-collapse-epa-science/

The Plight of Honeybees Shound Be A Concern for All... WGN TV 10:43 PM, MARCH 16, 2017, BY JULIE UNRUH, UPDATED AT 11:17AM, MARCH 31, 2017 Link: http://wgntv.com/2017/03/16/the-plight-of-honey-bees-should-be-a-concern-for-all-says-suburban-beekeeper/

The Continuing Plight of the Honeybee June 2, 2015 by John Diconsiglio Link: https://phys.org/news/2015-06-plight-honeybee.html

The Plight of the Honeybee – GW Today – June 1, 2015 Link: https://gwtoday.gwu.edu/plight-honeybee

Unique and Emerging Beekeeping Trends, Perfect Bee, February 29, 2016, Sarah Woodward Link: https://www.perfectbee.com/blog/unique-and-emerging-beekeeping-trends/

Just Add Love

I was reminded this week of a book I had read while working in the school Library. One of our special needs teachers had me order it in. After reading the name I had to give it a read: *The Boy Who Was Raised as a Dog: And Other Stories from a Child Psychiatrist's Notebook: What Traumatized Children Can Teach Us About Loss, Love, and Healing,* Dr. Bruce Perry and Maia Szalavitz

It outlines the experiences of working with emotionally stunted and traumatized children. Child psychiatrist Bruce Perry educates readers about how early-life stress and violence affects the developing brain. It was not an easy read, the stories of the children and what they had been through were horrendous, but fascinating. Dr. Perry is a North American expert who gets flown in for the worst cases. As the name portrays the stories are hard to read and the effects of the abuse and/or trauma on the children, gut wrenching; but unfortunately true.

Why do people do such horrible things to each other and worse yet – to children?

I know from my working with people that hurt children grow into hurt adults and unless they get the help they need to work through the deeply hidden pain that pain does not disappear it manifests in other ways.

The story told to me this week reminded me of this book:

A young lady, very troubled or on drugs came into a clothing store, she was obviously a lady of the evening. The first indication to the store clerk that something was off was that the young lady growled at her, much like an animal and then proceeded to start talking to herself while she perused up and down the clothing racks.

She spent a lot of time picking out clothes and putting them in a basket. Shortly after her arrival in the store, two other staff members approached the store clerk behind the counter and told her they needed to tell her about this particular young lady. Their body language betrayed their feelings towards the troubled young woman. They were not going to stand for her to be in the store and they were ready for a fight should she try to make a scene, steal or disturb other people. They literally glared at the young woman.

The store clerk behind the counter told the other two employees in no uncertain terms that the young lady would be treated with respect no matter what they felt towards her.

They were adamant that if the young lady mouthed off or stole something, the fight was on. The store clerk firmly replied that no matter what that young lady did, she would be treated with respect and if they could not, then to go to another part of the store. Three times she had to tell them that she would treat this troubled young lady with respect even if she stole from them because God would want them to. She explained that stealing would not be tolerated but respect would still be used. They could not handle this, huffed and made a bee line for the back of the store.

Unfortunately many people fall into this category.

The store clerk likened their attitude to the crowd of men that circled the woman caught in adultery in the Bible. Judging her and they were going to stone and kill her because of her "sin". This was the crowd to which Jesus said, "He who is without sin should cast the first stone," and the crowd slowly dissipated until no one but Jesus was left there. John 8:3-11

Why do we judge so harshly when we do not like what we see? Why do we worry about someone else's sin but not our own?

The young lady was in the store for at least 1 and ½ hours trying on clothes. Three sales staff rallied around her and helped her see what would be the best clothing choices, even if the clothing was somewhat scandalous. She confided to two of the clerks that she hated herself and her life, that she had no idea who her parents were and even wondered if she had a sister.

I thought of the above mentioned book when I heard this story because I wondered what kind of pain this young lady must have gone through to end up as a prostitute and to hate herself and her life that badly. She was obviously looking for attention and was getting all the wrong kinds.

The sales clerks had wondered throughout this whole process if this young lady had any money at all. She chose a pair of pants and a shirt that she wrapped around her head and shoulders so her midriff was totally exposed. She eventually wandered over to the checkout counter and confessed to the sales clerk that she had no money.

The clerk looked at this young lady and asked her what she could do to pay for the clothes if she had no money. She offered to come in, in a few days with money. The clerk said no. The clerk said how much was the clothing worth – they looked at the tags. She looked the girl in the eye and said, "If you have no money why were you trying on all the clothes?"

Without batting an eye the young woman said that the clothes she had on were covered with peoples "stuff" and yucky.

While her stomach lurched at what that statement really meant, without batting an eye the sales clerk nodded back and said, "I see. Well what can we do about payment?"

The young gal looked around and said, "I can work. I can sweep."

Seizing the moment the clerk said, "Perfect! I will get a broom and you can sweep for me for the clothing."

The young gal swept the floor, oh it was not a great job, probably not even a good job, but sweep she did.

And you know she walked out of the store with her dignity held high and feeling like a respected person, because she paid for her clothing with work. She was not shunned or felt to be put down. She even hugged the sales clerk on her way out and thanked her.

Smiling through her tears, the sales clerk watched her go, praying for her as she went.

She knew that the bigger picture was this: The store was not going to heaven, but the people God sends to the store sure are and if God sent this one, then who was she to treat her differently than anyone else.

My Mom, Lost in the City

My sister got a call around 6 on Sunday saying that my mom could not be found in the Care home she was in. They had called my sister, no answer, my brother, no answer and then my sister again, she answered and then she called me.

Mom is 83, has severe Alzheimer's, and a bad knee. When we questioned the home they said she had only been gone a little while and they heard a care aid found her a block away and was bringing her back. They told my sister this. I was told the care aid called the police and they were bringing her back but she had not been gone long.

When I questioned them further they seemed to not have answers, things like 'I did not take the call so I don't really know" would come up. For me after the call, I knew they really did not know where my mom was or how long she had been gone. Chances are they missed her at supper, 5:00 and that was when they realized she was gone.

I got off the phone knowing that they actually did not know where mom was, it was 29 degrees outside never mind the horrible smoke that hung over the area. My mom was out in the blistering heat wandering with her bad knee and little walker in the Lower Mainland.

I proceeded to call the Police department in that area of Vancouver and chose the department closest to her building. The operator I talked to said they did have a woman matching my mom's description turned in and the police officer had found her and called the paramedics who had taken her to the hospital. The receptionist did not know her name as yet. I tried to ask more questions but she guided me to call the hospital to confirm if it was my mom or not.

I called the hospital and after a couple of tries and getting hung up on I got through to the emergency department. They indeed did have my mom (she remembers her name) and yes she was safe. The Dr. had not seen her yet and she had only been there about 30 minutes.

I burst into tears when I knew she was safe and the intense relief that washed over me and the gratefulness that someone had found her was enormous. My fear level had been over the top as I felt so helpless to be able to help my mom. My finding her had taken less than 10 minutes. It made me so thankful to think that strangers will stop and take in the plight of other people. Without random strangers we would have lost my mom to ???

This is the 2nd time my mother has been turned in by a random stranger. It makes me think twice if I want to rush past someone who is obviously struggling.

I let my sister and brother know, my sister was already on the highway to get over to see her.

My sister found my mother resting, but seemingly calm and relaxed. She did not have on her knee brace, bra, or glasses. She had packed up her little walker with all her family pictures and she had headed out. A random passerby noticed that mom seemed confused, had called 911. Mom was found 2 kilometers away from the home. The paramedics and staff at Burnaby General were so kind to her. The Dr. had checked mom over and he was astounded at how well mom had done, although he found she did have pneumonia on top of it all.

In my heart I know that God was watching over my mom. He had to have been it is the only explanation that I have for how she got so far without her knee giving up (she has had 3 falls in her room in the past 3 months), no glasses to see, she is very hard of hearing. Never mind the smoke, traffic, heat, someone or something was watching over her.

I called the Care home to let them know I found my mother. They kept insisting that mom was only gone a little while, and that she had not gone far. They were not prepared for the blast when I told them that mom was far from the home and she obviously had been gone a long time along with having pneumonia (my dad died from pneumonia at this same home). Mom was released back to the home that night, with antibiotics for the pneumonia, she was hungry and thirsty.

I called the home the next morning and asked how mom was doing, well they must have been waiting for my call, mom was up and dressed complete with bra, glasses and knee brace. She had had her morning dose of antibiotics and they were very sorry for what happened the day before.

I accepted their apology. I told her that I was not looking for peoples jobs but that I would be reporting this incident to the management because I believed the problem was a management issue and obviously the wander guard system that was supposed to prevent people from leaving was not working, residents' lives were in jeopardy.

Today my phone started ringing with management. There is a formal investigation into what happened and I guess we will find out. For my mom it is not too late but what about the next time for my mom or one of the other residents?

As we journey on this earth we are supposed to be God's hands and feet, helping others as we go. Please consider when you are rushing by other people on the sidewalks and you notice someone seeming a little off, please take the time to find out if they need help – you could be helping someone's relative, like mine.

The Elephant in the Room

The laws of the land have been established for our protection and safety and I do not think many of us would disagree with that. We have law enforcement folks that are in place to uphold those laws. We follow those laws because we believe they have our best interest and the best interest of others in mind.

There are natural "earth" laws: gravity for instance; you can be sure if you throw something up, it will come down. Electromagnetic laws that say compasses will point "north". These laws are also "static" meaning they do not change.

There are "spiritual" laws that we do not often think about. If we believe that God created this universe and world and He says there are spiritual laws then regardless of whether we believe in them or not and they are still valid and in place, "static".

For instance: God says there is a heaven and hell and just because we cannot see them does not mean they do not exist. He also says there are forces at work around us even if we cannot see them. It has been my experience that people have no problem believing in demons and the devil and many believe in angels. Getting some people to believe in God, can be a different matter.

This week I heard a life lesson story where a person learned a valuable lesson of ignoring a spiritual law. We get in danger when we only remember parts of a law or parts of a Bible verse instead of looking at the whole phrase.

The scripture I am thinking of is: *"Submit yourselves then, to God. Resist the devil, and he will flee from you."* James 4:7

My friend ran into this principle while they were working out of town. They forgot the first part of the scripture, "submit yourselves to God" a spiritual law followed by "resist the devil, and he will flee from you." Many times we get it backwards, we chose to tell satan to get lost while ignoring God in the process.

My friend while out of town, isolated from their peers, and accountability friends, their church and their family, bunking with someone not on the same page. They were on their own in the midst of a strange town. This person did not think they would have any problems. Because of the awkwardness of bunking with another person they did not heed the spiritual law, "submit yourselves then to God" and tried to live their life on their own principals and it did not turn out so well.

I believe that satan loves to get believers separated from the other believers. He takes great delight to single us out one by one and watches for the opportune time to strike. He struck at my friend at a moment of weakness and now my friend and their spouse will have some consequences that will have to play themselves out in their marriage.

God gave us this spiritual law, "submit first to me" then.... "resist the devil" but too often we try to resist the devil and not do the first part, thinking we can handle life alone.

God gave me a picture of what this "would" look like.

Only after we have done the first part of the law can we expect to resist satan. Just what does "submit to God" mean? We have to go to the Bible, the spiritual law book for an answer; stay close to Him, to get to know Him so intimately that we know when we have wandered away.

We are the little mouse and we run to the gigantic elephant (God) and only when we are hiding under Him, can we turn and look at evil and say; "na na you cannot touch me". It is only when we are in the protection of the Mighty God of the universe because then and only then will satan and his helpers stop in their tracks and back off. They do not want to mess with the elephant in the room.

The Cluster Circle of Codependency

I had to work at not being codependent, it took years of counselling, books, praying and care groups to help open my eyes to what codependency is and how not to live in it.

As the word describes Codependent is a term used in dysfunctional relationships where one or more people/persons support or enables another persons' problems. Another term used for it is "relationship addiction".

What kind of things are we talking about enabling: alcoholism, drugs, gambling, mental health, hoarding, pornography, anger, sexual addiction, control, abuse, irresponsibility, immaturity, jobs, homework, to name some. (I added homework from my stint in the library, wow are there some codependent parents who try to give their kids an excuse for everything).

Usually the person/people who are enabling are only trying to "help" the other person - the one with the problem, their heart has the right motives but they are not actually helping. Instead they get tangled up in the mess and the person they are "helping" never has to take responsibility for their own problems.

It can be one to one relationships or larger groups: families, churches, boards, work places. In the case of family dysfunction it could be "this is the way we have always done it" meaning this is a generational pattern. Dysfunctional families or groups have members filled with fear, anger, pain or shame that is ignored or denied. Dysfunctional families' never talk about the pain or the problems, they learn to gloss over them or push them inward into themselves creating a havoc of other problems.

The sad thing is that often we do not recognize that the enablers are as emotionally wounded as the person they are helping. Codependency is a relationship that is emotionally damaging and can border on abuse. Codependency destroys happiness, home life, work life, and relationships. Codependent people believe they need to self-sacrifice their needs for the sake of another to "help them".

I call the codependent lifestyle as a cluster circle. The person I am trying to help is a mess, usually some kind of addiction is involved and I get tangled into the mess "trying" to help so I get just as caught up in the addiction because I am too close. Cluster circles go around and around and around for years and even longer. They continue until one person decides they are going to break the circle.

Typical pattern: person with addiction does what they do, they cause damage to themselves and others with careless words and the abuse. The enabler gets wounded in the process and says careless words, or says nothing, sadness or depression prevails. The addicted person says "I am so sorry, I will never do that again". The enabler believes the addicted person because it is said so sincerely and we live happily for a short while until it happens all over again. The cluster circle.

How do you know if you are codependent:[1]

1. You feel responsible to solve other people's problems.

2. You offer advice to others whether it is asked for or not.

3. You expect others to do what you say.

4. You feel used and unappreciated.

5. You try to please other people so you can feel loved or appreciated.

6. You take everything personally.

7. You feel like a victim.

8. You often use shame, guilt, manipulation to control others behavior.

9. You are willing to lie to yourself or lie to others for the addicted person's behavior.

10. You fear rejection and being unlovable.

If you recognize any of the above behaviors in yourself it might be also wise to ask these next ten questions:[2]

1. Do you avoid confrontation?

2. Do you neglect your needs to attend to another's first?

3. Do you accept verbal or physical abuse by others?

4. Do take responsibility for the actions of others?

5. Do you feel shame when others make mistakes?

6. Do you do more than your share at work, at home or in organizations?

7. Do you ask for help?

8. Do you need others' validation to feel good about yourself?

9. Do you think everyone's feelings are more important than your own?

10. Do you suffer from low self-esteem?

I have heard many sermons and teachings on, love your neighbor as yourself or you must serve and you must look after others that I had forgotten one basic flaw.

In the following scripture that is the guideline for all "loving":

"Love the Lord your God with all your heart, soul and mind. Love your neighbor as yourself." Matthew 22:37

The huge flaw is this question – where does the "self" come in?

We are so busy helping fix and help others that we forget ourselves in the process.

Wrong! Just like on an airplane the announcement says "You must put on your own oxygen mask first before you go to help others." How can you help others if you are not healthy or in the case of the airplane – dead?

Jesus taught us some really healthy boundaries to follow to prevent Codependency. Jesus was NOT codependent. Some might view Jesus as Codependent because He poured Himself out for others, which He did when He died on the cross, but that was something He choose to do.

Jesus was selfless, He was a servant, He cared deeply for hurting people, He did try to fix hurting people.

Oh dear, sounds like a contradiction to the top of the blog – right? NOPE. Jesus loved in a healthy way.

Jesus was selfless but He only took His orders from His Father, not people. He never got absorbed into other peoples "stuff". Codependency lifestyle is driven by the demands and lifestyle of others.

Jesus was a servant but He only did things that helped other people better themselves. He was not a doormat

[135]

and He had boundaries. He took care of Himself. He rested, He ate, He prayed and spent time with God.

Jesus cared deeply for other people but He did not excuse people for their sin. He called them on it with truth. He let consequences happen for behaviour. He did not enable them. Codependents feel they need to give excuse after excuse for other people's behavior.

Jesus tried to fix hurting people by offering them life with God and truth. He did not chase them down if they did not accept it. He respected people's choice and let them walk away. Codependents try to force others to do things "their" way – which is a form of crazy making.

If you have gone down the 2 lists above and you had a light bulb go off and you suspect you might need some help in a few areas – Good For You! That is Awesome!

That is the first step.

Some things to do:

1. Pray and ask God for direction.

2. Seek out a counselor and take the lists with you.

3. Seek out some good friends who will help keep you accountable to decisions you make.

4. Go online to the website in the footnotes or google Codependent

5. Pick up some great reading at the Library – *Boundaries* by Henry Cloud and John Townsend; *The Dance of Anger* by Harriet Lerner; *Codependent No More* by Melody Beatty is a classic or *Women Who Love Too Much* by Robin Norwood

6. Seek out a self-help group and there are many great ones out there: Al-anon, Al-ateen, Narcotics Anonymous. Addictions Centers have family support groups for all kinds of addictions. Mental Health offices often offer support groups. Christian based recovery: Celebrate Recovery, Freedom Session, Griefshare, DivorceCare. Pornography: Pure Life Ministries, Pure Desire Ministries, The Conquer Series is for men and they have a series for women who have addicted spouses.

7. Do not go through recovery alone, You are NOT alone and Codependency would love for you to believe you are – do not believe it for a second. There is help out there, God will direct you, go find it for your sake and the sake of those you love.

[1] https://www.recoveryconnection.com/top-ten-indicators-suffer-codependency/

[2] [2] https://www.recoveryconnection.com/top-ten-indicators-suffer-codependency/

Selfishness, Me and Margy Mayfield

Selfish: This word will conjure up some kind of image in your mind, either a person or event where someone proved to you that they were selfish.

Apparently when I was a teenager my siblings saw me as very selfish, only into my own thing, not really caring about anybody else's things. I probably was.

Years ago a lady who was my walking partner said something to me I have never forgotten – 'a person will either be a taker or a giver but you can never be both.' It has stuck with me.

As I have matured over the years I have had to do a lot of work on this one. It is easy to be self-centered. It is where 'me', 'I', only matter; a taker. I live in my little bubble of a world and if I decide to step out or let you enter in, it will be at my and only my discretion.

The problem is that when we live this way, the world collides with our bubble. There is no life in this world where other people or events will not come into our bubble. This can create havoc, anxiety or even anger on behalf of the bubble dweller.

Selfishness is ugly – no other word for it.

A person who lives a selfish life has no real time or energy to spend on behalf of others. If it is convenient for me then I might expend myself if you need help or something from me. Other people can spot a selfish person from a long way off and truth be told they would rather head the other way than hang around them. It can be painful to live with someone who is only concerned about themselves, the conversation centers around the "I" and rarely do they ask about "you". These kinds of people rarely pick up the phone to call you and see how you are; you do the reaching out to make the connection if it is going to happen.

Interestingly, the givers will read this and wonder if the selfish person is them; the takers will read this and know it is definitely "not" about them.

The Bible tells us that they will know we are Christians by our "fruit". That is what do others see in our life, how would they describe us? Do we leave a trail of good behind us, do people feel better when they have been in our presence?

I got a compliment a few weeks ago and it made me realize, that maybe I have some "fruit" trailing behind me. I do not think the person who said it realized how important what they said was to me. It is so important, that I cried when I came away from the conversation because it is how I want to live my life. I know I still have lots of work to do on this one but God gave me a glimpse.

They said, "I love spending time with you because you always make me want to get closer to God."

I love that, if I can share my life with others and leave knowing they are on a journey to getting closer to God, then my life will be full.

I heard a testimony the other day that rocked my world. It rocked my world probably for reasons other than you would think.

It was the testimony of Margy Mayfield. Margy is woman just like the rest of us, nothing super human about her and yet she changed the lives of many in just one day.

Her day starts out like any other she was headed out to do some errands. God had her meet her fate in a parking lot of K-Mart at the hands of a wanted serial rapist and murderer. He was on the FBI's most wanted list for 10 years, keeping one step ahead of the law and killing women in the process, he had just killed his last victim 12 hours prior to meeting Margy.

Margy's story is incredible and supernatural all at the same time. Her testimony is about 35 minutes long. One of the most fascinating listens you will hear.

Her story rocked my world because I hope I am like her. I want people to see Jesus in me and I want to be faithful to God to not judge others by what my eyes see.

Link to Margy's Testimony:

http://withusisgod.org/2009/07/margy-mayfield/

** End Note: Stephen Morin was killed by lethal injection in 1985 in Texas. Margy went to see him in prison just before he was executed. The warden cried at the thought of Stephen dying because Stephen had led many in jail to be saved. The warden himself said he was a Christian but Stephen taught him the real Jesus.

We Got A Miracle, Mom's Moved

We got a miracle – Mom is moved!

The thing with Alzheimer's is that the person will not remember what they did a few minutes ago even if someone treated them horribly and that makes elder care for people with dementia or Alzheimer's so hard. They cannot tell you when things are wrong – at least with their mouths.

My mom, I believe, tried to tell us something was wrong when she escaped from her care home on August 6. She had packed up all her pictures (and she had a lot) and taken them with her and off she went, escaping from the care home in Burnaby on a sweltering 29 degree hot and smoky day.

If you read my blog from then you will remember that a passerby called the RCMP when they noticed mom on the sidewalk. Bless them! She was 2.5 km from the home.

Well here we are a month later and we have had our miracle. God has answered our prayers, my mom is now transferred into a lovely care facility in White Rock. We were told that transfers take up to 4-6 months as you get placed onto the waiting list. We were told that there was no way we were getting her into the place in White Rock because it had a 2 year wait list.

They do not know my God.

Mom ran away twice, even though it was a secure facility where residents cannot get out – Ha! (another resident got out the day before I got there for my visit in August).

Our list of complaints: mom ran away, the care home missed mom's pneumonia; on another occasion, Mom got punched in the face by another resident; she had 3 falls where the care staff found her on the floor, we do not know for how long she had had to lie there since the room checks are spotty. My sister took mom down to supper one night only to find mom's spot in the dining room, her spot since 2012, gone. A lady came out of the kitchen and said they were told mom got transferred – does this mean she had received no care at all that day? Mom could not tell us of course, she would not have remembered.

I spent a week sitting and watching at the care home, it was one of the most frustrating experiences because I could not change a thing. I had to leave mom still there when I left. I sat in a parking lot and cried.

I was so discouraged, there seemed no way to move mom quickly, I had expected God to move my mom the week I was there. He did not and discouragement set in. The wheels were turning way to slowly for me. It was when I flew over the Rockies on the way home that I got a better perspective. The Rockies always melt my heart, they are so beautiful. Even though they were barren and dry, they are an incredible sight. I laughed to myself on the plane looking down, that if God can make these majestic mountains, surely, He can handle mom's move. That was Saturday on Monday I got the call.

The care home did some big blunders while I was there and it helped our "cause". One day there was no charting for mom recorded; we had no idea if mom had received her medications at breakfast or lunch and that staff member was gone to even ask. That was the day mom was wearing someone else's clothing. Then the day I grabbed the "floor" wheelchair to take mom out for a drive and it had feces (poop) on it and they just cleaned it off with a Kleenex and put a towel over the cushion for mom (no sanitizing) well they pretty much sealed the deal with me as I forwarded the picture I took of the wheelchair to Licensing at the government.

My brother and sister asked if I would continue in my quest to get "answers" and push for a care home inspection now that mom is transferred, my answer is "yes".

The problem at the care home is lack of management and training of staff; they fired all their long term staff last year and replaced them all with casual workers, to save money. The slide in care began. People's lives and health should never be put into the "bottom line" category. There are 300 beds in that facility and those dear souls cannot speak for themselves, many do not have family who even come to see them or monitor their care. A good percentage of them are veterans, people who put their life on the line to help defend others and our country. Our country should make sure they are taking care of them.

We got our miracle to get our mom out, but what does that mean for the others left behind?

Just as that anonymous passerby took notice of our mom's plight on the sidewalk and got help, I feel the need to do the same for those others who cannot get their voices heard.

What in your life appears to be a Mountain: something that will not move, or seems insurmountable? Change your perspective, go into nature and look around and then give this Mountain over to the God the one who can build mountains and tear them down.

Walking Right Through

Today I got a light bulb vision. I love those because they are a word picture in my head that help me understand the topic even better.

We were listening to our friend tell us about her trip to Hungary. It was a dream of hers and she enjoyed every moment of it.

One of the things that stood out to her was a room in a church they had gone to visit. The above picture is one of the portions of that room. This architect had heard that a princess was coming for a visit. He wanted to do something special so he built her this breathtaking room. It took him 1 year and 9 months to complete his work.

Just looking at the picture you can tell it is a work of art and a labour of love.

Well the princess came and rushed through the room, ignored it and went straight to another part of the church.

How utterly sad! I imagine the architect was heartbroken.

It was just after that the analogy flitted into my head.

How often do we rush right past the things that God wants us to notice? He worked, planned and prepared something just for us and we went right on by because our eyes were not looking for "that". That was not our "expectation".

May we slow down and ask God to open our eyes to the beauty and gifts that He gives us and to stop watching for only the things "we want". May we be open to explore all the opportunities that we are given each and every day.

Almost Invisible

While in Vancouver a few weeks ago I had an opportunity present itself that caused a decision to be made: act or ignore.

I was waiting at a Tim Hortons for my niece to come for a visit. I had gotten there a bit early and grabbed our lunch. While I was waiting I noticed a lady probably in her early 50's, sitting quietly at her table. I suspected that whomever she was with was grabbing the food and would come along shortly.

As the time continued, no one came. I love to people watch, so I started to watch her. I mean, of course, I did it discretely. I noticed that she had sat herself at a little table where the top of the wall was taller than she, so no one from the counter could see her, unless someone came around to wipe down the tables, the staff would not notice she was there.

It was a warm summer day and she was dressed with a little jacket, the morning could have been chilly when she started out, so nothing seemed abnormal, until I spied her footwear, tall warm winter boots, the fuzzy kind. Not really suitable for the days weather. As I pondered her, I started to wonder if she was homeless and was seeking a safe place. I could find "no evidence" besides the boots and the fact there seemed to be no purse, but not everyone carries one.

She sat very still, with almost a serene look on her face as if she was waiting for someone and then I noticed her head would nod down as she dozed off momentarily and then she would snap back awake.

When my niece came, who is a nurse, I told her that I was not sure if the lady was okay. My beautiful niece walked over and sat down, introduced herself and told her she was a nurse and that we were just checking to make sure she was okay.

She was amazed that someone would care and thanked us very much all the while saying she was fine. My niece came back and told me that this lady was more than likely on heroin especially with the nodding off.

My heart felt so sad for her, she was not young, but obviously alone. I wondered what her story was.

My niece and I had a marvelous visit together and then she left to go back to work.

I realized I had been at the coffee shop for 2.5 hours and that lady had not moved spots or even basically positions. No one had come to see her, no one stopped to talk to her. *She was almost invisible right there out in the open.*

In a world of 7.5 billion people how many remain invisible? We just do not see them.

As I gathered my things I stopped at the lady's table and sat down. I told her that I had been there a long time and noticed that she had had nothing to eat or drink. I asked if I might give her some money to buy some food. She reacted almost wildly to the thought. So I then asked if I might buy her some food. She took more to this idea but still refused. It took some convincing but she agreed to a bowl of chilli.

I went to the order line.

I felt a hand on my arm as she appeared at my side.

"I feel so uncomfortable," she said. She continued on that she had not always been like this and it was just a matter of time until things got better. I could only nod, she was obviously embarrassed.

I told her that I did not want her to feel uncomfortable, it was certainly not my intention. She nodded but still looked afraid.

An idea came to me, "I believe God told me to buy you some food."

She took a step back to study me and think for a moment and then said, "May I have a coffee as well?"

"Of course," was my quick reply.

She returned to her little table.

When I carried the food over she could not stop thanking me.

I leaned down and said, "I truly believe God sent me here today to buy you this meal, remember He really loves you."

To which she grinned and started to eat her food, she seemed to understand or accept that.

I walked out with tears of gratefulness that I had had the privilege of blessing that lady. It only took $5.00.

I was blessed much more than she.

What if I had ignored the prompting? I would have missed my blessing, her blessing and a huge opportunity of helping someone who felt invisible be noticed.

It took me back to the random act of kindness for my mom, from whoever called for help when she was lost and wandering the streets in Vancouver back in August.

Learning to listen to those little inside promptings, those

inside nudges, we may never know the outcome but we just might change someone's life for an hour, a day or even longer.

Let's learn to tune in!

The Man Cold

I am sitting here listening to my husband moan and groan as he battles the "_man cold._"

He assures me that women cannot handle a man cold. Much like the tv commercial I am tempted to ask him if I should call his mother.

I am not sure how women continue on when sick, with the kids, the cooking, the chauffeuring and even their job. (I have so far resisted the urge to bring up child birth, probably saving that one for the clincher).
But there does seem to be a difference.

Perhaps, and again it is only my opinion, women are tougher. My groaning hubby is balking at this as he asks me to make him a cup of tea. (I'm giggling which is probably not kind).

Now given certain times and circumstances men are "stronger" but in other circumstances women are "tougher".

I for one do not relish changing a spare tire. I could if I needed to but I probably would take forever jumping up and down on the tire wrench to get those lug nuts undone, or have to give up and phone AMA.

I am glad to have men around to move certain items around the house that I can barely budge. Men are physically stronger.

I love to bounce plans for building or certain situations off of a man. Men are so logical and see things from an easier and interesting perspective that can make so much more sense. It's often a relief.

Do you think it is coincidence that each of the sexes is "tough" but in a different way?

Or was it designed by a planner who knew if we would just work together, value each other's strengths, and work amicably things could get done in a really efficient way?

I think that most of the time we roll our eyes because he/she does not see things our way and we argue over our differences instead of value them. We even see these differences laughed at on tv sitcoms.

I have worked side by side with my hubby doing renovations and our wood shop, admittedly we can argue over how to do a project or buckle down and get the job done, it truly depends on the day.

I think today I needed to remember that he can be "tough" and strong when it counts. Right now I have to take him his cup of tea.

My Weapon of Choice

I have not talked about prayer in any of my blogs yet, at least I do not think I have. How very strange because prayer to me is like breathing, you cannot live without it. As much as I need air to breathe, I need prayer to fill my soul with the connection to God.

As a whole, this world is all about "connections". We want the best connections, with the fastest service, free roaming and no hidden service charges. We are on our cell phones all the time, connected to wi-fi, connected to our friends, connected to our work, our families. We are such a connected world. Well God has the best communication system going, and it is NOT even new and it is always free, worldwide roaming and you guessed it, it is hands free.

You can be connected to the God of the universe 24/7 - it is called prayer.

Prayer to me is an ongoing conversation with God. It can be inaudible, that being, quietly in your head, it can be audible, speaking aloud with your voice. Sometimes it has requests, sometimes it has thanks, sometimes it has adoration and sometimes it is really more like me venting.

Often people only pray when they come to the end of themselves and there is nowhere else to go.

I think of prayer as a "weapon", it is my weapon of choice. The battle field is the world and it will try to beat you down. Life can get so very complicated, confusing and hard.

Prayer is the ultimate weapon because I am not venting to someone who cannot do anything about my problem. I am venting to the only one who can.

Oswald Chambers in his book, *My Utmost For His Highest*, has some of my favorite quotes on prayer:

1. Get into the habit of saying, "Speak, Lord," and life will become a romance.

2. We hear it said that a man will suffer in his life is he does not pray; I question it. What will suffer is the life of the Son of God within him, which is nourished not by food but by prayer... Prayer is the way the life of God is nourished.

3. We tend to use prayer as a last resort, but God wants it to be our first line of defense. We pray when there's nothing else we can do, but God wants us to pray before we do anything at all.

My Utmost Favorite:

4. Prayer does not fit us for the greater work; prayer is the greater work.

So I ask you, have you prayed yet today? Give it a try.

Richmond, Virginia

Richmond, Virginia that is where I was last week, it almost seems so long ago. Richmond is a large city of 220,000 people. We were surprised at how many businesses were closed down, gone, in the area around the conference center. We talked with a couple of people about the economic situation, it is not good. Their wages are not high and we toured a grocery store and noticed food prices on par with ours.

It is a beautiful city, the weather was amazing 24-29 while we were there, but it can get cold there too, we walked over to Belle Island, a 2.2 km island, on the banks of the James River, lined with walking trails.

There were remnants of old metal buildings. We read on a sign that the island had had several uses, once a nail factory, another was a fishery and most notorious as a POW camp for up to 30,000 Union soldiers in the civil war 1862-1865. A lot of soldiers froze to death over the winters apparently.

Richmond was the first capitol of the USA, the first legislative assembly sat there in 1631 – the city has history. History is one of those things, you cannot go back and change, if the past is not good, you would be better to use the past to enlighten the future, educate, guide and direct but you cannot change it.

Biggest graveyard I ever saw was there, we drove through it and were amazed at the size, it went on forever, we certainly did not see all of it. One small section has 18,000 Confederate soldiers buried there.

It is this city that had the riot over their historical monuments a while ago. They have a lot of statues and monuments all over the city and they have one street called Monument Avenue, this is where all the action happened.

The city's mayor: Levar M. Stoney, an African-American had this to say about the riots and statues:

"As I said in June, it is my belief that, as they currently stand without explanation, the confederate statues on Monument Avenue are a default endorsement of a shameful period in our national and city history that do not reflect the values of inclusiveness, equality and diversity we celebrate in today's Richmond.

I wish they had never been built.

But context is important in both historical and present day, perspectives. While we had hoped to use this process to educate Virginians about the history behind these monuments, the events of the last week may have fundamentally changed our ability to do so by revealing their power to serve as a rallying point for division and intolerance and violence.

These monuments should be part of our dark past and not of our bright future. I personally believe they are offensive and need to be removed. But I believe more in the importance of dialogue and transparency by pursuing a responsible process to consider the full weight of this decision.

Effective immediately, the Monument Avenue Commission will include an examination of the removal and/or relocation of some or all of the confederate statues.

Continuing this process will provide an opportunity for the public to be heard and the full weight of this decision to be considered in a proper forum where we can have a constructive and civil dialogue.

Let me be clear: we will not tolerate allowing these statues and their history to be used as a pretext for hate and violence, or to allow our city to be threatened by white supremacists and neo-Nazi thugs. We will protect our city and keep our residents safe." Mayor Levar M. Stoney

Racism is not dead, it is still a small ember that keeps getting ignited all over the country, we need to pray it gets totally snuffed out.

It is interesting to note that in the midst of all this we were there. 5,000 people from all over the world, people from over 2/3 of the worlds countries were meeting in the center of all this. It was the Aglow International Conference. We were there to band together in unity – color, country, cultures. The women and some men wore their traditional dress, beautiful, colorful and impressive. I could walk up to anyone there and know I had acceptance and they knew they did as well, it was like being at a very large family reunion. It was totally awesome!

The 5,000 people represented the leaders of Aglow in their country. I learned a lesson about the power of God inside a person. I could just walk by some of them and feel a power surge coming off them. It was a new experience for me, I tested it several times. I would get close, feel this power and then back away and resume. It was extraordinary.

I went up to one lady from Cameroon, commented, "You are a power house for God aren't you?" She looked incredulously at me and replied "Of Course!" Another from Kenya had an air of royalty about her as she sat and told me of her life journey and her deep deep relationship to God.

That is the difference, these folks knew who they were or more importantly they knew **"whose"** they were. Their life amid, chaos, poverty, strife was founded on a deep and solid relationship to God, unshakable faith. Some of the people I talked to were persecuted for their faith, life was not easy, and yet their deep faith flowed out of them. I was humbled.

The whole conference was amazing as was the trip and I am so blessed and thankful to have been able to go, to be part of something so much bigger than me and my small corner of the world.

Spiritual Giants or Regular Folks?

In a world that makes us often feel like we do not fit or that we are not good enough, pretty or handsome enough, rich enough, it is so very good to know where we can go to find others just like us.

I am about to give you a list of what the world would call "failures", you know those people who probably would not amount to much in life: (at least from some people's perspectives)

- Adam and Eve broke the rules and then lied and hid

- Abraham lied and pimped for his wife

- Sarah laughed at God and disbelieved Him

- Moses stuttered and was a murderer

- David's armor did not fit, he was too young

- Hosea's wife was a prostitute

- Jacob was a liar and wrestled with God so his name was changed to Israel (he who wrestles with God)

- David had an affair and was a murderer

- Solomon had 700 wives and 300 concubines

- Job was a whiner

- Jesus was poor

- Abraham and Sarah were too old to have babies

- Lazarus was dead

- Naomi was a widow

- Ruth was an outsider

- Rahab was a prostitute

- Jonah ran away from God

- Gideon and Thomas doubted God

- Jeremiah was depressed

- Elijah burned out and wanted to die

- Samson had long hair

- Paul was a murderer

- Noah got drunk

- Timothy was too young

Philip Yancey says: "You learn a lot about a person by the friends he selects, and nothing about God is more surprising than His choice of companions."[1]

Yes the above list of names are some of Gods favorite people, it is a list from the Bible, some of our spiritual "giants." So you see, you and I are in good company, if God chooses to call these folks "friends", and the fact that He used those people mightily to serve Him, there is hope for us.

The coolest thing is that God used them before, *get this please,* **before** He asked them to change, shape up or measure up – God accepted them just as they were – faults and all. You see that is who God is, He loves us, you and me other people as they are. His whole goal throughout all of the Bible, from cover to cover is to have a relationship with people. It is totally not about "religion", with its finger pointing rules; it is all about "relationship" - ours and Gods.

I have heard and observed over the past few years that folks do not think the Old Testament is relevant in today's society and world. I have had to question this.

Most of the names mentioned on the list are from the Old Testament. It is the Old Testament that gives us the history of the world, civilization and cultures. It has wars, famines, murders, songs, poetry, sex scenes that should make you blush and promises to hold on to. It reads a lot like some of today's newspapers, the Old Testament contains a lot of "real life." How much more relevant can that be?

In the world of today, where so much around us does not make sense, where private lives are exposed and exploited on the media, where the media is exploited for political biases, and we wonder just how are we supposed to live, who are we supposed to believe and we try to blunder along on our own. It is refreshing to read the above list and sit back and breathe a sigh of relief that God's got this, He knew the faults of "those" people and He knows yours and He absolutely loves you anyways. He used messed up people in the past and as a matter of fact called them "friends" – this should give us a sense of relief but also a sense of wonder to just how God might be able to use you too.

Will you let Him?

[1] The Bible Jesus Read, Philip Yancey

A Heap of Lovin'

We find it hard to want to Bless other people, you know those drivers who cut you off or change lanes without signaling; what about that one that stole the parking spot you had been patiently waiting for?

What about those grouchy, miserable people you run across at the store, at work, at school or just about anywhere?

Oh come on, admit it, you did not want to offer blessings their way....

I was at the movie the other night; the movie was "Same Kind of Different as Me". I really loved it, an awesome movie based on a true story. The movie digs into some things that often people would love to forget: racism, homelessness, pride and prejudice.

But if I had to give a one word answer what the movie was about, I would say: Love.

Love: the little word and actions that can change the entire world.

There was one line in the movie that penetrated into my thought processes and there it remains.

Scene:

Man is escorting his drunk alcoholic father to the car after his father had been rude and obnoxious to his family at the dinner table. The man tells his father that he never wants to see him again as he shuts the door after him.

The other guest on the stairs watching the scene says, "God bless him" as he watches the man's father drive away.

The man looks at the guest and say's there is nothing good in his father.

The guest looks after the car and comments, "There is a kind man hiding deep down there. Sometimes you just have to Bless the Hell Out of Them."

Oh I love that phrase, WE (you and me) have to Bless The Hell Out of Them!

For starters, we cannot change anyone, but God can and do you know how God does it? He loves them and He Blesses the Hell right smack out of them, love wins every time.

Love always wins. People do not stand a chance when you love them.

When we were in Richmond, Virginia we came across a couple of people who needed a little lovin':

We were waiting for the trolley to come and pick us up for a citywide trolley tour. As my friend and I were standing on the sidewalk, a middle aged man approached us. He came up to us and said that he was embarrassed but he wondered if he could ask us if he could borrow $11. He was in town to work on a movie, he was the assistant director and not a bum asking for money, he had just left his wallet at the hotel by mistake. He promised to pay us back. He had a passport to show us that he went to the Caribbean every winter and he was fully employed, just was in need of $11. (I am still wondering why $11, it is such an odd number). His story went on for at least ten minutes. My friend and I were fully engaged over his story, we tried to avoid eye contact with each other as it caused the corners of our mouths to start to develop into a possible giggle.

Now that might sound mean (the giggle) but from our perspective the man was trying "way too hard" to convince us that he was not a panhandler. His lengthy liturgy was a bit of overkill to the situation. His shoes did not portray the look of a working man, nor did his teeth or at least the ones he still had.

We listened intently to his story and at the end of it (I had already decided what I was going to do) but I told him that we had listened patiently to his story and now he could listen to ours. I proceeded to give him the short version of how God loved him. He absolutely rose to the occasion and then graced us with another 10 minutes of how much he loved God, went to Sunday school as a child, every Bible story and scripture he could remember, it was truly awesome.

I laughed when he came to the end and took out a $20 and handed it to him with the words, "Here you go, God told me to give you a $20 a long time ago". He looked concerned and then asked me where would I be tomorrow so that he could pay me back. I again laughed and told him he did not have to as long as he would remember that God loved him. He said that was easy and off he sauntered.

Another day as we were roaming the streets of Richmond looking for a restaurant for lunch and noticing that so many of the stores and businesses were closed and empty I approached a young black lady in her early twenties, her name was Aketa. I asked her why so many businesses were shut down. She told us that economics in Richmond were not good. It was then that I noticed her sign beside her that said "out of work", she was looking for donations. I had totally missed the sign, but that was fine with me and we continued our conversation. She informed us that in order to "panhandle" in Richmond you had to have a permit, they only allow so many panhandlers in the city and yes you paid for the permit (seriously!). If the police came around and you did not have a permit they whisked you off to jail, which I mean, go figure, they are going to feed and shelter you in there anyways, so what is the problem? The whole thing seems silly to me.

We talked for quite a while with this young lady and left her with some money and a Bible. She was so elated over the Bible she jumped up and hugged us. She blessed us probably more than we blessed her.

Love is free and we can offer it at any time to anyone we come into contact with, why not give it a try today and see if you can Bless the Hell Out of Somebody today! It will probably make a great story!

Snuffleupogus and Other Healthy Things

My time in the Health Food industry was a really fascinating time for me. Although it is now interesting for me to watch people currently catch on to things we were saying 20 years ago.

For instance: We promoted Probiotics way before it became main stream to do so, we called it Acidophilus back then. Probiotics are your good gut bacteria, they are very important to your overall health. There are many strains or different kinds of good or healthy bacteria.

The fact that we used to call Probiotics as Acidophilus, reminds me of a fun story.

I had hired a lady to work for us at the health food store who was such an amazing people person but she needed a bit of training on the products. I was in the back room and she came to the door with a deer caught in the headlights kind of look across her face. She said that she had a customer out front who was asking if we had any "Snuffelupogus". I did a double take and tried to figure out what she was asking and then I started laughing – to anyone not knowing about Acidophilus, the closest and most popular word at the time was Sesame Streets 'Snuffelupogus". I still laugh about that one.

I had it explained to me that taking Probiotics was like saying I drive a car, a generic term.

Taking Acidophilus and Bifidus was like saying I was driving a ford car.

Taking Rhamnosis or Streptococcus thermophiles was like saying I was driving a Ford Explorer.

There are many different strains of Probiotics just like there are kinds of cars. Each strain works on different areas of your digestive tract. Getting a good probiotic with many different strains is best.

You can lose your good bacteria by taking antibiotics. Antibiotics do not recognize good and bad bacteria, they wipe it all out. Unfortunately good bacteria does not grow as fast as bad bacteria so to give your gut a boost it is recommended to take some good bacteria or Probiotics along with and after you finish a course of antibiotics. You should not take the antibiotics and the Probiotics are the same time, but wait 3-4 hours in between. I usually recommended people to take a full bottle of Probiotics after a course of antibiotics to ensure they got their healthy bacteria back up.

What often happens: you finish a round of antibiotics and 2-3 weeks later the same infection rears up again. This is because the bad bacteria grew faster than the good and now you are re-fighting the same germs again. You need to boost the good bacteria with Probiotics. Quite honestly the amount of Probiotics in "yogurt" is not enough to help you after a course of antibiotics, you will need to get the pill form which is much more concentrated (don't buy enteric coated).

Since cold and flu season is just around the corner I thought I would give you my favorite cold and flu chasers:

1. Occicilium – Homeopathic, safe for everyone, including children. This is Europe's #1 flu fighter. Europe has 3 stages of medical intervention: #1) homeopathy 2) herbal 3) antibiotics. Homeopathy is a whole other blog article but it works, is safe for everyone. You can find it in most drug stores and health food stores now.

To take Occicilium, the best way is right at the beginning of a cold or flu, if you feel something might be trying to attack you, take it! The package contains little plastic vials filled with tiny pellets. You open up a one vial and dissolve all of the pellets under your tongue, they taste like nothing. If I am getting a cold/flu I will take these right away, usually 3 times on the first day and then 2-3 on the 2nd day and most of the time I do not get sick. They can stop colds/flu right away. For little ones you can dissolve the pellets into water and drop it into their mouths.

2. Olive Leaf – capsules. Olive leaf is a natural antibiotic, antiviral, antifungal. I used to give it to my entire family one a day when cold and flu season started. If they started to get sick, I upped it to 2 or 3. I have only found Olive leaf in health food stores up to this point.

3. Oil of Oregano is certainly an option. It just tastes awful. You can get capsules or liquid and if you cannot swallow either, you can rub the oil into your skin and it is absorbed in that way but be warned you will smell like Italian food or pizza for the rest of the day. Available in drug stores and health food stores.

There are many other options that are standby's for other people but these are mine.

The Hard Questions

Do you struggle with any of these questions: evolution versus creation; or where do dinosaurs fit? Aliens and UFOs? Can the Genesis story actually true? Are there dragons? How do birds fly?

If you have these kind of doubts, you are certainly not alone. The majority of Christians do not know how to answer these questions.

There is a group of dedicated people who can answer all that for you, and they would LOVE to come and teach you.

Creation Ministries International is an organization whose primary outreach is sending out speakers to churches to build Christians up in their faith. They are a group of not for profit ministries in several countries around the world united in their vision of educating people on these very topics.

You do not have to take my word for it – check out their website: https://creation.com

These folks are the scientists, Doctors, historians, experts whose life work is to find those answers and then give us the tools to answer the questions that stump us. They have over 10,000 written articles, magazines, over 200 videos, including YouTube, TV shows, books, DVD's and....speakers.

Right now, they are going across Canada speaking and teaching the Biblical facts and history proving the Biblical account of creation to be true.

Creation Ministries is coming to the Grande Prairie area in November.

Actually there are a whole lot of places they are coming to in the next little while: All over Alberta Tour, a British Columbia Tour, Manitoba, Saskatchewan, Nova Scotia and Ontario tours.

Link to their events page:
 https://creation.com/calendar

If your town is not on the list and you want a tour to come near you, just give them a call 1-877-746-3543.

Creation Ministries International is about much more than Canada – they are located in the following countries: Australia | New Zealand | South Africa | UK/Europe | United States.

Joy

I have a friend and this really did happen to her. She was standing on the step outside of church one Sunday and a gentleman was coming towards her from the parking lot. He stopped right in front of her and asked her if she had the joy of the Lord in her heart. She replied yes she did. He went on to tell her to move it up to her face and promptly left and entered the church.

I remembered that story when I read what Phil Calloway, a Christian writer and comedian, wrote about his father in law. The man did not want to know anything about God for years. His daughter, Phil's wife, kept trying to figure out what was the stumbling block. Finally one day he told her: "Christian's look like they got all the joy of life sucked right out of them." Frankly it was not something that held any attraction for him. Why would anyone want to walk around so miserable? Good question.

Now I am not going to lie, life is hard. There are speed bumps, moguls and mountains that often appear out of the blue. They happen to everyone at some point in life, it is not "if" they will happen but "when". The point of this blog is not to make you "smile and life is all good", the point is this: there is always a reason to smile, even amidst our pain and hurt.

If Christians have this amazing news that they are saved from hell, have an incredible relationship with the God of this Universe and can converse with Him no matter where they are....Why do Christians get the wrap of looking so miserable?

Perhaps it is because many of us are. The following is true of most of us in North America.

We have so much compared to many countries of the world and in spite of this we have bought into the "more" philosophy. Our media marketing forces us to watch ad after ad showing us how complete we would be if we only had "more". It leaves us feeling empty.

Then we have our "want it now" mentality: drive up food, coffee, banking, drug stores, photos, cleaners. If we need answers, we whip out our phones and call on Siri or Google for help, because they can connect us to anything we "need." Heaven help us if we have to wait for slow internet connection, it is as if the world simply stood still and we are not sure what to do with that.

With so much freedom, why are we so miserable?

David Martyn Lloyd-Jones, Pastor, Westminster Chapel in London wrote the book "Spiritual Depression".

"Christian people," writes Lloyd-Jones, "too often seem to be perpetually in the doldrums and too often give this appearance of unhappiness and of lack of freedom and absence of joy. There is no question at all but that this is the main reason why large numbers of people have ceased to be interested in Christianity."

There are no "Eeyores" in heaven. Nope, not a one. Part of who God is, is Joy.

Your problems are not making God wring His hands and complain that He is not sure what to do. He has a Plan! He has had a plan from the beginning, even before you were born. His is that BIG! His plan is to make people in "His image". That alone should make us excited.

Joy is so much different than Happy. Happy is from the "things" around you but "Joy" is strictly from God. Joy is a gift from God, it is a part of God Himself, it is one of the fruits of the spirit.

Kids get joy and perhaps we should spend more time with kids. Their world is serious but they seem to have a way to accept what is. I think this is why Jesus loved to spend time with the children.

Boy 4 years old: Mom what happens when your phone falls into the toilet?

Mom: Why?

Boy: Never mind.

Boy age 3: "Jesus was in the kitchen and He said I could eat a cookie." What the 3 year old said when caught with a cookie after he was told NO.

During a doctor's visit, the urologist asked my 3-year-old son to pull his pants and underwear down. When she went to examine him he looked at her and said "awkward". (Jessica Button)

A little boy recently informed me that squirrels eat acorns because they don't like Mexican food.

About halfway through a spaghetti dinner a 3-year-old asked what the green stuff on the pasta was. When told that it was parsley, she threw up her hands and said, "Well, I've never had it before, and now, my life is ruined." (Christine Horos)

One day my 4-year-old was upstairs and yelled, "ouch!" When I asked what happened he yelled down to me, "I stubbed my toe! The one that ate roast beef!" (Jenn Memolic)

We are approaching the start of the Season of Joy – the Christmas Season. No matter what is going on inside our world, the hurricanes that are swirling around us, there is nothing that can erase the joy of the first Christmas, the birth of a Savior. It truly is a miracle, a big fat joyous miracle, that cannot be erased or taken away, now that should move a joy smile from your heart and plunk it right up onto your face.

Go on... Smile and Share the joy!

Buddy

I believe that dogs, not people, are the closest thing to God's unconditional love, they love you no matter what, at least that has been my experience since I was born. There has always been a dog or two around in my world.

Last weekend, suddenly, we had to say goodbye to one of our two golden retrievers – Buddy.

Buddy and Buster are 9 years old, and they have been inseparable since birth; born to different moms, same dad and on the same day, they have never been apart. Punishment was to put them in two different rooms for 5 minutes. They would greet each other like they had been apart for years!

Funny story: when I went to "looking" for a puppy, I only had the intention of buying 1 dog. Brian and I were only dating back then, but I brought him with me........

We pulled up to the farm and 11 little puppy heads shot up over the boards in the dog pen and Brian right away said "Can we get them all?" I should have known then to turn the truck around.

We picked 2 out of the 11 to decide on and the owner said to bring those 2 into the house away from the pack to watch and play with them for a while. I ended up choosing Buster and Brian said he would take the other puppy back out to the pen. I paid for the 1 puppy, picked him up and walked out to the truck. As I got close to the truck I could see Brian in the cab with the other puppy. I walked up to the truck and Brian locks the truck door and says through the window, "You had better pay them for 2 if you want that one, because this one is coming with me."

That is how I got 2 puppies, best decision ever.

I wanted to share a couple of "Buddy" stories with you.

Buddy was an American retriever which meant he was stockier and a working dog. He wanted to retrieve; there was never a more excited dog than Buddy when he was retrieving. If he was not retrieving, chances are he would be chewing on one of his toys. We had to invest in "hard" not chew-able toys. Buddy liked to rip apart "soft fuzzy things". It was horrific for little children if they came over and had a "stuffy", Buddy always thought it was for him. The child would unfortunately hold the stuffy high in the air and run, and the chase was on. Child running and screaming, Buddy chasing, tail wagging and me in hot pursuit yelling "Don't run!"

Buster is an English retriever; bred more for show, longer hair and he does not mind telling you that it should be "petted." While Buster liked to retrieve for a short time, Buddy was our endurance runner. Buster would much rather be "sniffing" than retrieving. If Buster wanted to play then he would run after the ball with Buddy but then he would run back attached to Buddies tail or leg, trying to get him to slow down and let him get some of the credit for retrieving.

On one of our adventures up to Liard Hot Springs, Brian and I stopped in at a campground along the way. We were going to cook supper over the campfire and sleep in the car for the night. The campground was well off the highway 20 kilometers or so and very isolated, we drove around scouting out the area. We came across only one other vehicle in the whole campground. It seemed very odd to us and we took notice of it because it was an older van backed into the path that one of the outhouses sat on; backed right up next to it, like in the bush. Now these were not "newer" outhouses, they were older and stinky so we wondered why would someone be parked that close to one? Possibly an accessibility problem for the person, you know not able to walk or something?

We decided to go away from the van to another area and proceeded to make our fire. We were cooking our food and the dogs were running around sniffing everything.

All of the sudden Buddy walked to the back of our vehicle and sat down and started "growling" at the bush. Golden retrievers are not mean dogs, they do not growl, usually wanting only to "play". This was very startling to both Brian and I. It was not a growl we had ever heard before, it was an intimidating growl. Buster took notice and then plunked himself right down beside Buddy and started to growl as well. We noticed that the dogs had perfectly placed themselves between us and the bush. We both scanned the bush and listened but other than the growling, we could hear nothing. It went on for quite a long time and it became unsettling. Brian looked over at me and said "Do you want to leave?" I nodded and he said, "Me too!"

We packed up and left, the dogs that whole time never left their sentry positions between us and the bush and kept growling.

We drove by the van on our way out of the park a good hour to hour and a half later and it was still backed up next to the outhouse. We could not drive away fast enough.

Once we got into cell service, we called the RCMP because something did not sit right and reported the van. We got a call back from the RCMP sometime in the night on our drive home thanking us for the call, they had gone out and the person in the van had been doing some illegal activity was all they said.

Brian and I believe that Buddy saved our lives that night; had we gone to bed locked in the back of our car with "bad guys" out in the bush, who knows what could have happened. We never again doubted the dogs "instincts" about people.

Yes Buddy has left a permanent hole in our hearts, Buster is missing his brother badly, we will recover but it will not be the same. Buddy was one of the "good" ones, even if he and Buster did eat all 24 butter tarts at Christmas one year, including 6 foil tins.

We are so grateful for his unconditional love, we will miss him.

My Husband's Favorite Picture

This is my husband's favorite picture: his little hot head.

Let me fill you in on the picture because I do not think I have shared the story with you before.

This is my wedding day picture. Brian and I got married in a hot air balloon!

It was absolutely wonderful. I had been in a hot air balloon before and fell in love with it. For Brian it was a stretch because he has a "height" thing but as he discovered, unless you hang over the edge of the basket and look straight down, the height thing does not matter. You look out, not down.

When you book a balloon flight, you are not guaranteed that you will fly that day since ballooning is very dependent on the wind. The wind cannot be above 13 km/hour. But we booked it and showed up at 7:30 am in the dark and the cold (October), the pilot said to us, "You must have an in with someone we have not been able to fly in over 2 weeks because it has been too windy, but today is perfect." Thus began our flight.

We had about 30 people come to see us off at Muskoseepi Park while the crew was inflating the balloon. It was fun to have people around us to celebrate and get excited for us as the balloon got bigger and bigger along with our anticipation. It took about 45 minutes for the crew to get the balloon up and ready to fly.

The balloon basket does not look "big", but 5 of us fit in there just fine: the pilot, the pastor, our best person (Martha), the bride and the groom.

Martha was 80+ at the time, a little nervous about heights as well. She is very special to Brian and I and she was our best-person/witness. She could not figure out how she was going to climb into that basket even with the little stool and it was beginning to cause her some anxious thoughts. While her back was to Brian, he just scooped her up in his arms and gently placed her in the basket. She giggled the entire time.

We climbed in and the crew let the ropes go and we started to float. What an incredible feeling, nothing scary, very smooth in motion and truly delightful. We ascended above the crowd of well-wishers below, above the trees, above the city all the while pointing out landmarks. The balloon does not go high enough to block out the landscape below, you still can point out buildings and places.

I have to report, we made balloon believers of Brian, Martha and Pastor Glenn. As a matter of fact, halfway through the flight I asked Pastor Glenn who was enamored with the balloon ride, wearing a little boy grin the whole time, if we were going to get married during the ride. He was so thrilled with the balloon ride and finding out from the pilot all the techy things about the balloon he almost forgot why we were there.

We had our wedding ceremony way up in the sky with the pilot and Martha as our witnesses. It was absolutely the best wedding ever!

As we sailed the skies we were graced with trumpeter swans, geese flying around us, we saw deer and moose below us, it was as close to magical as you can get.

The balloon is subject to the winds and so you cannot plan on which direction you are going to be heading. The wind on the ground could be blowing a different direction than the one you find higher up, so landings are not pre-planned. Traditionally the first hot air balloons in France carried champagne with them to offer to the farmers or frightened spectators below when they landed. Turns out the frightened French farmers often used to pitchfork the alien from the sky and pierce the balloon fabric making them useless. They were appeased when the pilot offered them champagne and the tradition still carries on today. When you land you are treated to a traditional champagne (or orange juice) toast.

On the ground there is a ground crew chaser van following the balloon at all times to be there for when you land. We also had our friend Steve follow us and be there for our arrival as well and take us back to our cars (the crew would have done this as well).

To land the pilot looks for a field or opening on the ground big enough to safely land the balloon, no power wires, fences, or buildings too close together. In our case he knew the farmers who owned the plot of land we were going to land on and he brought us down basically in their front yard. He had warned us that sometimes the basket could fall over on landing and to not hold the basket with your hands holding the outside or your fingers could get squished. I have to admit, there was never a more protected person than Martha when we landed, snuggled between Brian, Pastor Glenn and the pilot, she was completely safe. Divinely helped, our pilot landed us totally straight up and the basket did not tip so it was not an issue.

Our flight was just over an hour long and it was glorious, I would highly recommend that you add a Hot Air Balloon flight to your near future.

And that my friend is the rest of the story to my husband's favorite picture.

Real versus Imitation

In my newest book *The Complete Love Circle,* it opens with the following story and it got me thinking about Christmas.

The Pearl Story:

A little girl, 4 years old out shopping with her mom at the local department store. They got near the checkout area which was filled with various kinds of kids treasures and candy placed at eye level to draw all children's attention.

The little 4 year old spotted a plastic pearl necklace hanging right in front of her face.

"Ohhh, can I get this mommy? Please can I get this?" she exclaims.

"Not today honey," Mommy answered, placing her groceries up onto the conveyor belt.

"But I love it. Please mommy, pl…ease!"

"Not today mommy said."

"I want it Mommy please!"

"Tell you what," Mommy countered back, "why don't we leave it today, and you can do some jobs around the house and earn the money to buy it. When you have enough money saved, we can come back and buy it. Okay?"

Sadly the little girl looked longingly at the pearls but nodded her okay with her head.

The little girl worked hard around the house and earned the money for the pearls in 3 weeks. They went back to the store to purchase the plastic pearl necklace.

True to her word the little girl "loved" the necklace and wore her plastic pearls every day. Faithfully every night she would slide them off her neck and carefully place them beside her bed before she went to sleep.

Daddy would come in and say prayers with her and kiss her good night. One night daddy said to her, "Honey, would you give Daddy your pearls?"

Shocked at the question the little girl wide eyed with amazement just shook her head and answered, "No Daddy, oh no!"

Daddy just smiled and kissed her good night saying, "That's okay honey. Have a good sleep. "

Every night Daddy came in to say good night and at least once a week he would throw out the same question, "Honey would you give Daddy your pearls?"

Each time the answer was the same. This continued on for about 2 months.

One night Daddy came into the bedroom and the little girl was sitting on her bed sobbing.

"Honey what is the matter?" Daddy rushed over to her concerned.

"Ohhhh Daddy..... here," the little girl choked out amidst the sobs, she thrust out her little hands and lifted up her pearl necklace to give to her treasured possession to her Daddy.

What the little girl did not see was that each time Daddy asked her if he could have her pearls, his left hand always slid into his pocket on his pants. Tonight as Daddy reached out with his right hand to take the offered up plastic pearls, his left hand came out of the pocket with a small but long and slender box that had been in his pocket each night he came into say good night.

"Honey," Daddy said, "Daddy loves you so much, I never wanted you to have plastic pearls, you are much too precious to me, I want you to have "real" pearls," and he placed the new box with the new and precious pearl necklace into her hands. *

God never has plastic for us, never the imitation, He has true treasures and He is waiting to give them to us. Perhaps we do not recognize them or see them as important.

Like a lot of things in life, Christmas can be one of those times, I get caught up in the plastic Christmas instead of the real. I start thinking of all the things yet to do on my to-do list and wonder if I will be able to get "all" those things done in time.

My list: make a list, shop for presents, bake the sought after Christmas treats, write my cards, mail my cards, decorate the house and the tree, wrap the presents and get the best and biggest turkey....

I tend to forget that Christmas will come whether or not I am ready; because Christmas is not about me or my list at all.

I like to substitute my choices, my plastic pearls into my Christmas plans, thinking they are the "real" thing. But God, God wants us to have only the real, precious and priceless treasures.

[184]

God's version of Christmas was a baby born in a stable to an unwed teenager while she and her fiancé were on a trip to another city. It was a pretty big deal to God and so He sent out His angels, His heavenly host, to go tell folks about it. God sent them to the shepherds - those smelly guys out watching the sheep in the fields. He never told the Mayor, the important business people, the church or the surrounding neighbors; and yet, this baby would change the world for all eternity. A true treasure.

It got me to thinking that perhaps, my version of what seems important at this time of year, truly isn't. What's your Christmas based on real or imitation?

*Excerpt from: The Complete Love Circle - A Bible Study, Jane Wheeler, 2017

90 Minutes in Heaven

I read a book by Don Piper - *90 Minutes in Heaven*. Don is a pastor and he was declared dead and gone for 90 minutes in a horrific automobile accident. Don spent those 90 minutes in heaven, while his physical body lay dead and covered with a tarp in his wrecked automobile. It is an incredible story of what he witnessed and saw, it makes me long to see heaven (but I will wait).

When Don came back to earth after the 90 minutes, he came back to a life of constant pain and a very broken body. His first 2 years were filled with more pain than he thought human beings could stand. He has endured more than 34 surgical procedures; he still lives in chronic pain. Don is so honest in his story, he talks about his fight with depression, the "why's" of the pain and the why he was sent back to earth. He came to the conclusion that he was supposed to share his story and bring hope to other people by recounting his experience in heaven. His purpose is to share his heaven encounter and instill hope of something better to come, reveal that heaven is for "real" and offer encouragement to other hurting people.

I love that Don has spent the remainder of his life, trying to help other people make sense of non-sensible things and to offer them hope. Things that cause heartache, physical pain, mental pain, the unexplainable events of life that tumble in, around and on us. Don does it well and has helped so many other people find hope and encouragement to continue their life journey when they wanted to give up.

If you want the low down on "heaven" you will have to get a copy of his book, no one can tell it like Don, but I can tell you it excited me to the point of reading the book twice and then listening to the book on CD. The book instills hope and the incredible strength of humans to withstand things they never thought they could.

I will share one of my light bulb moments of this book: The fellow who prayed for Don to come back to life, in the wrecked car, and Don were in a coffee shop, sometime after Don's recovery. The other fellow started to cry. He himself had gotten a light bulb moment. He explained to Don that he realized for most of us, if we saw someone standing in front of a speeding car or a child run out in front of one, we would not even hesitate to rush to them and push them out of the way, possibly harming ourselves in the process. Most of us would not even think, it would be in our nature to do so, we would "react". But he noted that in this world, every day, we are surrounded by hurting people, people in crisis and pain, people jumping off the cliff of suicide and we sit by and say nothing about the God who can help them. He realized that most of us are not doing our part to bear one another's burdens, to share the hope we have with others.

This was my light bulb, am I sharing the hope I have with other people? Am I telling them there is a heaven waiting? Am I leaving them with a hope that there is a better way to get through their pain? That there is a God who cares and other people who will love them? I get so caught up in my own selfishness that I think I miss many opportunities to offer a listening ear, a comforting word or even just a hug of encouragement. I want to do better, Don makes me want to do better. God makes me want to do better and one other thing makes me want to do better....

Let me share one other light bulb moment with you, one that I think at this time of year will fill you with a sense of wonder to want to find out, "really?"

Don says that the most "impactful" thing for him about heaven was the sounds. The one sound that he can close his eyes and still hear, the one sound that for him describes heaven, the one sound he aches to hear again - is the "swoosh" of angels wings. He said the sound is like nothing you have ever heard, but so intensely wonderful it takes over your being, and it is only one of the sounds of heaven.

Don recalls : "Heaven was like a first-class buffet for the senses. It felt more real than anything he had ever experienced before."

And that my friends is my one other thing that makes me want to do better: I Want To Hear the Swoosh of Angels Wings.

As we sing our Christmas Carols: Angels We Have Heard on High, Hark the Herald Angel Sing, and Angels From the Realms of Glory. I Want To Hear Them Swoosh.

Angels are real and so is heaven and from that heaven came a baby, not just any baby but a baby named Jesus, the Savior of the world, that the Angels sang about and swooshed over.

This Christmas season, let us rejoice and sing along with the angels and if you dare, close your eyes and listen so very carefully, perhaps, just maybe, you will hear a strange noise that could be considered a "swoosh."

My Christmas Blog

God is hilarious. No I truly mean it. I have found His nature to be so out of the box, that I am astounded each time He shows up with a unique turn of events, something that defies logic or a scratch the head, how can that even be, moment. God is not stuck on doing things "normally", not at all!

The Bible is filled with these unique and mind bending events.

Noah's Ark – the people of the land had never seen rain, so imagine what they thought when Noah starts to build an Ark. The animals came to the Ark, no rounding them up - that's a go figure.

Jericho – the walls fall down after the army marches around the city 7 days in a row, blowing trumpets.

Moses – leads the whole Israelite nation out of Egypt after he goes to talk to Pharaoh – Moses stutters

Moses – leads the whole Israelite nation through the middle of the Red Sea – the Sea parts and they walk through on dry land

Jonah got swallowed by a whale.

Israel gets saved by a prostitute.

A shepherd "boy" kills a giant warrior with a sling shot.

Balaam has a talking donkey.

Daniel survives the lion's den.

Shadrach, Meshach and Abednego survive a fiery furnace and the king and attendants see 4 people in the fire but only 3 are put in and come out.

I cannot make this stuff up, it is in the Bible and all of these are out of the box scenarios.

I personally think that humor in heaven is to watch us humans experience these mind blowing experiences and God grins over our reactions.

And now we are about to celebrate the birth of a baby, His name is Jesus. Not an ordinary story here either, but really after reading the Old Testament and seeing all of these other stories, why would we even think that God would do anything "normal" here. I think the above stories were just God setting us up for the "big" one.

Mary the virgin teenage girl gives birth to Jesus. The Bible says Mary became pregnant by the overshadowing of the Holy Spirit. She did not become pregnant by a physical act, it was spiritual. Jesus was born to a virgin. How is that for an out of the box scenario?

The Birth of Jesus

This is how the birth of Jesus the Messiah came about: His mother Mary was pledged to be married to Joseph, but before they came together, she was found to be pregnant through the Holy Spirit. Because Joseph her husband was faithful to the law, and yet[e] did not want to expose her to public disgrace, he had in mind to divorce her quietly.

But after he had considered this, an angel of the Lord appeared to him in a dream and said, "Joseph son of David, do not be afraid to take Mary home as your wife, because what is conceived in her is from the Holy Spirit. She will give birth to a son, and you are to give him the name Jesus, because he will save his people from their sins."

All this took place to fulfill what the Lord had said through the prophet: "The virgin will conceive and give birth to a son, and they will call him Immanuel" (which means "God with us").

When Joseph woke up, he did what the angel of the Lord had commanded him and took Mary home as his wife. But he did not consummate their marriage until she gave birth to a son. And he gave him the name Jesus."
NIV Matthew 1:18-25

Absolutely mind blowing. Folks have argued about the "virgin birth" since it happened: could it be? Couldn't be? Of course it could be, did you read the first part of the blog? God delights to WOW people.

What if I told you that what was true of Mary can be true for all of us? I almost saw you give your head a shake.

We too can have the direct act of God, God wants to come and dwell inside us.

Jesus said when He was taken up to heaven that He would not leave us alone, He would send us the Holy Spirit.

"... And I will ask the Father, and he will give you another advocate to help you and be with you forever— the Spirit of truth. The world cannot accept him, because it neither sees him nor knows him. But you know him, for he lives with you and will be in you." John 14:15-17

The Holy Spirit comes to live inside of us at our invitation, God will not force us, He is waiting for us to invite Him. This would be our second birth or spiritual birth otherwise known as "born again."

If you want to have this amazing relationship with God, it is simple, but only because it cost God so much (the life of Jesus), pray the following prayer: "God, I want to have a special relationship with you, I want you to be in my life. I acknowledge that Jesus paid for my sins when He died on the cross and I am ever grateful. I recognize that I cannot ever be good enough to get to heaven on my own, and I am totally blown away that you loved me and died for me even when I am not perfect. You love me just as I am. I invite you to come into my life. Please send your Holy Spirit to come and live inside of me, to share life with me, that I might never be separated from you again. I ask You to guide and teach me as we grow together. Thank you. Amen."

If you prayed this prayer, welcome to the "family". You are now a member of the family of God often known as a "Christian" – a follower of Jesus Christ. Mind Blowing isn't it?

Do not separate Christ from Christmas, step it up and like Jimmy Stewart in "It's A Wonderful Life" run through the streets shouting "Merry Christmas Bedford Falls", well... you could substitute your town's name, a person's name or just have some fun with it! Be out of the box – God sure is.

Merry Christmas Everyone!

A Component Called "Others"

The span between Christmas and New Year's is usually not quite as hectic as the weeks preceding Christmas. It is often a time where we can spend some reflective time to look over the past year, and look to the future to see where we are headed and make some goals and plans.

What if, in our reflective time we added a component to our plans, let's call it "others"?

What I mean by that is, there are people who you and I know who seem to have changed the world by their very presence. Actually we all change the world by our very presence but some of us have greater influence than others. I pondered, what is it about those ones who have the greater influence? I came up with the following conclusion: it is the component called "others".

The common characteristic of these people is they are self-less. They care less about themselves and more about the cares and concerns of others. Mother Teresa was a prime example.

In our North American culture today, we have stuck pretty close to the saying "looking out for number one". Now looking out for yourself and your family is not wrong and human instinct kicks in naturally. But as I was looking at the faces of the people shopping in the stores these past couple weeks, they are anything but happy, in fact, many were down right miserable.

Listening to the students in the library all last year, listening to others around me, and then in Richmond, Virginia at the International conference I attended, hearing the worldwide epidemic of "hopelessness", well it just has me thinking.

What if looking out for the betterment of "others" actually makes you happier and gives you hope? You be the change; now there is a thought and possibly a goal...

I want to share this story with you.

In Papua New Guinea there is a man, barely 5' tall, so you could not say he "stands out in the crowd" but actually he does.

In 1981, Wionare Mitimu completed grade six in the Eastern Highlands where his father worked as a missionary. There was little hope of going on to high school because his family could not afford the school fees.

In 1994, he started training as a "preschool" teacher. This involved learning how to use local languages in preschool education. In 2003, he was called to Ukarumpa in the Eastern Highlands where he started a two year course called "Strengthening Tokples Education in PNG" or STEP.

Wionare went on to use his training to train others to become preschool teachers, but not just in populated places. His students and his dedication took him to some remote places on the whole planet, in Papua New Guinea. Wionare has spent his life training others.

Wionare started training 20 preschool teachers, then another 20 and in total he trained 67 preschool teachers. 27 of those teachers were from his own language group and those 27 each started their own preschool. It takes a year to complete the training.

Did it make a difference?

"Some of his students are training to be pilots....One of my former students is a surgeon at the Goroka Hospital. Two girls are studying to be teachers at the University of Goroka. Another girl has graduated as a nurse. They are all my students. They come from my village."

One of the things that astounds many people who come to learn about Wionare's feats, is that none of the preschool teachers he trained get fortnightly salaries like their colleagues in government and church run schools.

"They don't get paid money. The community gives them a house, makes their food gardens for them. The community supports them.

"Every six months, the people give them a small cash compensation they collect in a bilum. Then at the end of the year, we make a small kaikai and say 'thank you' to them."

The preschool teachers do not get "paid" – let that sink in for a couple of moments.

Wionare started out "stuck" in life. Money poor, rural and rugged climate, not fully educated, he did not have the opportunities that most of us have, but he had "heart".

Do you feel "stuck" in life? Wondering how to put purpose and meaning into something that you do? When you are pondering about next year, why not put a component called "others" into your plans? There are so many volunteer opportunities around, so many people needing help and hope in their life.

Who knows, by mentoring or helping just one other person, you get the benefit of purpose and meaning and you *are* being the change that this world needs.

*Wionare's full story:

 https://inspirationalpapuanewguineans.wordpress.co
m/2017/10/19/wionare-mitimu-bible-translator-who-
established-27-tokples-preschools-trained-67-teachers/

About the Author

Jane Wheeler lives in the oil town of Grande Prairie, Northern Alberta, Canada with her husband and golden retriever. Jane has three grown sons that bring joy, excitement and sometimes lots of prayer to her life.

Together with her husband they create amazing wood furniture and other treasures in their little woodshop.

God sees Jane as a teacher, leader, writer and builder. When she is physically not building in the woodshop, you will find her building into the Kingdom by teaching, speaking and writing as God leads and directs her.

You can connect with her on her website where you will find her contact page and a link to her weekly Wednesday Blog: *Midweek Moments* plus a list of other resources she has available.

If you wish to sign up to get her weekly blog emailed to you, please send a note on the contact page.

Website: http://www.rayofsunshineministries.com